How To Lose Friends & Piss People Off

A Satirical Guide to Becoming Everyone's Least Favorite Person

DAAJAN BAIN

Copyright © 2025.

All rights reserved.

No part of this book may be copied, reproduced, stored in a retrieval system, or transmitted in any form or by any means—electronic, mechanical, photocopying, recording, or otherwise—without prior written permission from the author, except for brief quotations in a review or academic reference.

This book is a work of humor and satire. Any resemblance to actual people, living or dead, real-life situations, or events is purely coincidental. If you find yourself relating to the chapters a little too much, well… that's on you.

Peachester, QLD 4519

ISBN: 978-1-7636631-6-9

First Edition, 2025

For inquiries, collaborations, or to send passive-aggressive feedback, contact: deebainauthor@gmail.com

DISCLAIMER

This book is purely satirical and meant to be taken in the spirit of humor and absurdity. While *How to Lose Friends and Piss People Off* dives into a collection of exaggerated behaviors and questionable tactics, it's not intended to be a literal guide or serious advice.

The scenarios and tips within these pages are designed to entertain, provoke laughter, and maybe even inspire a little self-awareness. If you recognize yourself (or someone you know) in any of the examples, remember it's all in good fun. The goal here isn't to encourage bad behavior but to shine a comedic light on the habits and quirks that can sometimes make social interactions... let's say, interesting. However, if you find yourself relating to a few too many chapters, it might be time to consult your therapist, a trusted friend, or at least someone who can kindly remind you to dial it down a notch.

Please don't actually sabotage friendships, alienate loved ones, or dominate conversations—unless, of course, you're ready to deal with the consequences (or buy them a copy of this book as an apology).

Enjoy the chaos, laugh a little too hard, and, above all, keep in mind that no friendships were harmed in the making of this book. *Probably.*

CONTENTS

Introduction	1
Chapter 1 - How to Make It All About You	3
Chapter 2 - How to Be Offensively Late (Every Single Time)	7
Chapter 3 - The Blame Game	10
Chapter 4 - How to Be the Ultimate Couch Surfer	14
Chapter 5 - Steal Their Thunder & One Up Their Stories	18
Chapter 6 - Be The Friend Who Always Needs a Loan	23
Chapter 7 - Splitting The Check Fairly Is a Rookie Mistake	27
Chapter 8 - Be The Expert at Everything	32
Chapter 9 - The Top 10 Worst Ways to Apologize	37
Chapter 10 - Turn Every Outing into a Photoshoot	42
Chapter 11 - Terrible Listener Tips	46
Chapter 12 - How to Complain About a Gift	51
Chapter 13 - How to Ruin Secret Santa	55
Chapter 14 - Master the Art of Being Unreachable	59
Chapter 15 - Turn Movie Night into an Argument	63
Chapter 16 - Be Generously Selfish	67
Chapter 17 - How to Weaponize Honesty	71
Chapter 18 - Win Arguments, Lose Relationships	75
Chapter 19 - Real Life Scenarios	79
Chapter 20 - How to Be an Emotional Blackhole	85
Chapter 21 - Make It Weird: Crossing Every Boundary	90

Chapter 22 - The Behavioral Dynamics of Social Sabotage Study	94
Chapter 23 - How to Be a Nightmare Co-Worker	98
Chapter 24 - The Vacation Saboteur	103
Chapter 25 - Be the Ultimate Party Clinger	107
Chapter 26 - How to Piss People Off in Everyday Situations	111
Chapter 27 - Sabotage Every Game Night	116
Chapter 28 - Steal the Chair of Power	121
Chapter 29 - How to Ruin a Wedding (As a Guest)	126
Chapter 30 - Mastering Disengaged Body Language	131
Chapter 31 - How to Make a Terrible First Impression	136
Chapter 32 - How to Be a Spectacularly Ineffective Leader	141
Chapter 33 - How to Rope Someone Into Doing Something	146
Chapter 34 - The Art of Never Letting Them Escape	150
Chapter 35 - How to Ruin Bathroom Etiquette	154
Chapter 36 - The High Maintenance Sick Person	158
Chapter 37 - The Couple That Should Have Broken Up Ages Ago	162
Chapter 38 - How to Make Every Meal Unbearable	166
Chapter 39 - Quiz: Are You a Friend Losing Champion?	170
Chapter 40 - The Social Saboteur Awards Ceremony	174
Chapter 41 - Redemption	178
Chapter 42 - Survival Guide for Collateral Damage	183
Conclusion	187
Acknowledgments	
Glossary	

INTRODUCTION

Have you ever looked at the people in your life and thought, *"Wow, I've got way too many friends"*? Or ever wished your friends and people in general would just leave you alone? Good news—you've come to the right place. This book is your ultimate guide to trimming down that pesky social circle, creating awkward family gatherings, and making office environments so uncomfortable that even HR keeps their distance.

So, what can you expect? In the pages that follow, we'll cover every obnoxious behavior, cringeworthy habit, and hilariously self-serving tactic you need to become the person people actively avoid. From mastering the art of interrupting every conversation to nailing the "Oh no, I forgot my wallet" during dinner outings, we've got you covered. By the time you finish this book, you'll be well-equipped to dominate social interactions and alienate even the most patient of friends, family members, and coworkers.

But here's the kicker: while this book is undeniably tongue-in-cheek, it also holds up a mirror to the little things we all do sometimes. Maybe you'll recognize yourself in these chapters. Maybe you'll see a friend, sibling or co-worker and suddenly understand why your last group dinner, family holiday, or team meeting ended in strained smiles and awkward goodbyes. And who knows? You might even walk away with a renewed sense of self-awareness, or not—that's totally up to you.

Most importantly, remember to have fun with it. This book is meant to be light-hearted, absurd, and a little over-the-top. Whether you're reading it for a laugh (or using it as inspiration to secretly improve your own social skills), gifting it to a friend, family member, or someone who *might* just need a hint, ... welcome aboard. Let's dive into the wonderfully disastrous world of losing friends, annoying family, and pissing people off.

1
HOW TO MAKE IT ALL ABOUT YOU

Congratulations! You've taken the first step toward alienating everyone who's ever cared about you. To utterly lose friends and piss people off, you've got to master the fine art of self-absorption. Why waste time listening to others when you can talk endlessly about yourself? Why bother being interested in their lives when yours is clearly so much more fascinating? Remember: every conversation is an opportunity to remind people just how incredible (or tragically misunderstood) you are.

Step 1: Hijack Every Conversation

No matter the topic, steer the conversation back to yourself. Are they talking about their promotion? Great! That's the perfect segue into the time you almost got promoted but didn't. Are they sharing an exciting story about their vacation? Interrupt them with, "That reminds me of the time I went to [insert vaguely related place here]!" Bonus points if you can make your story longer, more dramatic, and slightly better than theirs.

Pro Tip: Don't even pretend to listen. Instead, nod distractedly while mentally rehearsing the next thing you're going to say. When they finish talking, jump in with, "That's nice, but wait till you hear this!"

Step 2: Always Be the Victim

Your life is hard, and everyone needs to know it. If someone dares to share their struggles, make sure they understand that yours are so much worse. Did their car break down? Tell them about the time yours broke down in the middle of nowhere, during a thunderstorm, while being chased by wild animals. After all, as Mark Brandon (Chopper Read) famously said, "Never let the truth get in the way of a good story." It doesn't matter if the story is true, the point is that your suffering must always be more significant.

Pro Tip: Use phrases like, "Wow, I wish I had your problems," or "Must be nice to only have that to worry about." This ensures they'll think twice before confiding in you again.

Step 3: Downplay Their Achievements

Nothing says supportive friend like minimizing their hard-earned success. Did they just buy a house? Yawn and say, "That's nice, but the market is so overpriced right now. Good luck with that mortgage." Are they thrilled about a new relationship? Raise an eyebrow and mutter, "Hope they're better than the last one." The goal here is to plant just enough doubt to keep them from getting too confident.

Pro Tip: If they confront you about your negativity, act shocked. "What? I was just being honest! Don't you want my opinion?"

Step 4: Refuse to Celebrate Their Wins

When a friend achieves something great, your job is to remind them that it's not *that* big of a deal. Did they finish a marathon? Mention how your cousin once did an ultramarathon… barefoot… in the snow. Did they land a dream job? Casually bring up all the horror stories you've heard about that industry. The key is to ensure that their moment of joy is overshadowed by your indifference.

Pro Tip: If you're feeling extra bold, use social media to subtly diminish their achievement. Comment on their post with, "Didn't know they were hiring anyone these days. Congrats, I guess!"

Step 5: Treat Group Settings as Your Personal Stage

Parties, dinners, and gatherings are the perfect venues for showing everyone how much more interesting you are than them. Interrupt conversations, dominate the spotlight, and don't let anyone else get a word in. If someone tries to share a story, one-up them immediately. If they start to lose interest, crank up the drama. Tears, exaggerated hand gestures, and shocking revelations are all fair game.

Pro Tip: When someone else inevitably gets fed up and leaves early, loudly ask, "What's their problem?" This ensures everyone knows you're the victim in this situation.

Reflection Exercise:

Think back to the last time a friend shared exciting news with you. Did you:

1. Genuinely celebrate their success?
2. Listen attentively and ask follow-up questions?
3. Hijack the conversation to share your own news?

If you answered 3, great job! You're already on your way to alienating everyone around you. Keep up the splendid work.

By now, you should have a solid grasp of how to make every interaction revolve around you. Remember, self-absorption isn't just a bad habit; it's a lifestyle. Master this chapter, and you'll be well on your way to achieving your goal: losing friends and pissing people off with flair.

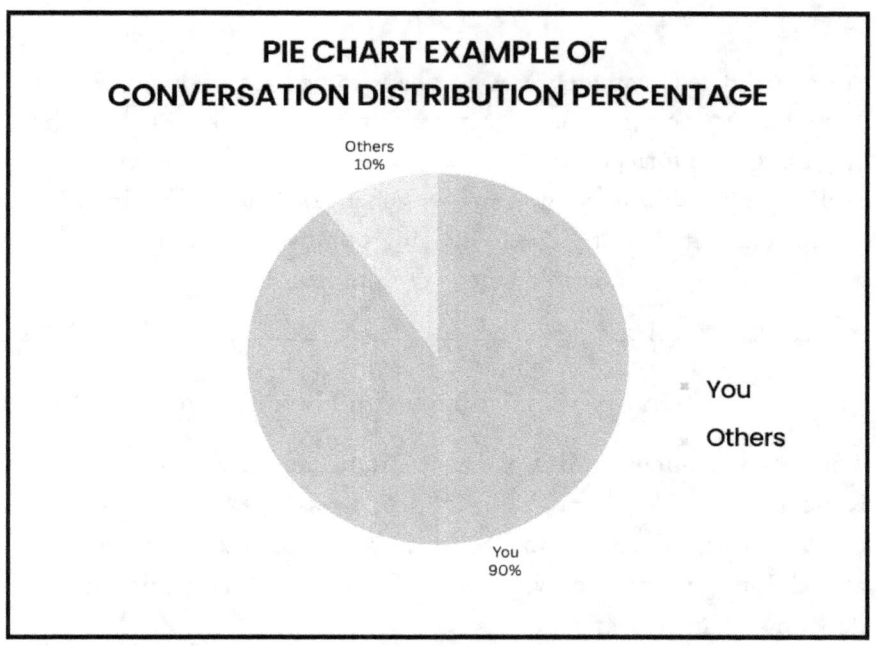

2
HOW TO BE OFFENSIVELY LATE (EVERY SINGLE TIME)

Punctuality is for amateurs. Who needs to be on time when you can be the chaotic force that disrupts every gathering, keeps everyone guessing, and turns even the most relaxed brunch into an emotional rollercoaster? If you want to master the art of being offensively late, this chapter is your guide to arriving not just late, but gloriously unapologetic every single time.

Step 1: Text "On My Way!" When You Haven't Even Left Yet

This classic maneuver ensures maximum irritation. The beauty of this tactic lies in its false hope. Your friends, foolishly believing your "on my way" text, will start scanning the horizon for your imminent arrival. Little do they know, you're still at home in your pajamas debating what to wear.

Pro Tip: Add an ETA to your message for extra flair, like, *"Be there in 10!"* when you know full well it'll take at least 30 minutes just to leave the house.

Step 2: Arrive Dramatically, Pretending It Was Impossible to Be on Time

When you do finally show up (a solid 30-45 minutes late, ideally), don't just stroll in like nothing happened. Make an entrance. Sigh loudly, throw your arms in the air, and launch into an elaborate tale about the insurmountable obstacles you faced just to grace them with your presence. Apologizing is optional, your sheer presence is apology enough.

Example:

"Oh my gosh, you wouldn't believe the traffic!" (There wasn't any.)

"I couldn't find my keys anywhere—my dog must have hidden them!" (You don't even have a dog.)

Pro Tip: Act offended if anyone expresses frustration at your lateness. Say something like, "You have no idea what I've been through today," and shift the conversation back to you. If food has already been served, inspect everyone's plates and exclaim, "Oh wow, you guys started without me?" as though they should've been happy to starve waiting for you.

Step 4: Bonus Move—Leave Early

If you really want to solidify your role as the least dependable friend, don't just arrive late— leave early, too. After making everyone wait for you, spend about 20 minutes complaining about how *packed* your schedule is. Check your watch dramatically, sigh, and declare, "I hate to do this, but I really have to go."

Pro Tip: Blame something vague but important sounding, like a *client call* or *work emails*. They'll never question it, and you'll look busy and important while dodging any real commitment.

Step 5: Normalize Your Behavior

The secret to making chronic lateness work is consistency. Be late so often that your friends and family just come to expect it. Make it their problem to plan around your inability to show up on time. If they complain, laugh it off and say, "You know me—I'm always late!" as though it's a charming quirk rather than an irritating habit.

Pro Tip: Flip the script. If someone gets mad about your lateness, act surprised and say, "Oh, I didn't think it was that big of a deal. Are you okay?" This subtle gaslighting will make them question their own frustration.

Reflection Exercise:

Think back to the last time you were late. Did you:

1. Apologize profusely and promise to do better?
2. Text a vague excuse about traffic?
3. Show up 45 minutes late with a coffee in hand and zero remorse?

If you answered 3, well done! You're well on your way to becoming a legendary latecomer.

Being on time is overrated. Why rush to be punctual when you can make everyone's plans revolve around your lack of planning? By following these steps, you'll never waste another moment worrying about clocks or schedules. After all, the best plans are the ones where you show up last and leave first.

3
THE BLAME GAME

Accountability is exhausting. Why take responsibility when you can simply make someone else the fall guy? Owning up to mistakes is boring, and apologies are for suckers. In this chapter, you'll learn the tactics for shifting blame with style, ensuring that every mishap in your life becomes someone else's problem—preferably your friends' or coworkers'. Whether it's a spilled coffee, a missed meeting, or an existential crisis, there's always someone nearby who's clearly at fault. Let's dive into the blame game.

Step 1: The Spill-and-Blame Maneuver

Imagine this: you're riding shotgun in your friend's car, coffee in hand, when suddenly you hit a bump. Coffee spills everywhere. Whose fault is it? The cup holder's, of course! Or maybe the car's suspension. Or better yet, *your friend's driving*. Why were they so reckless as to hit that pothole in the first place?

Pro Tip: Don't just blame them; double down. Say something like, "I told you your car's cup holders are useless!" Bonus points if you insist they clean the car themselves.

Step 2: The "You Should Have Reminded Me" Defense

So, you missed an important deadline at work, and now your boss is fuming. The obvious solution? Blame your coworker. After all, isn't it their job to keep track of your tasks?

Say, "Why didn't you remind me? You *knew* I had that report due today!" If they counter with, "I'm not your assistant," roll your eyes and mutter something about how true team players would've checked in. Shift the focus to their supposed negligence and let your own forgetfulness slide quietly into the background.

Pro Tip: Use passive-aggressive guilt to seal the deal. Say something like, "I thought we were in this together," followed by a dramatic sigh. That'll teach them to question your priorities.

Step 3: The "I Was Just Following Your Lead" Act

Here's a fresh twist: blame your mistakes on bad advice or influence. Did you mess up a project because you skipped steps? Easy fix— claim you were just following their suggestions.

Say, "Well, you *did* say I should take a shortcut. I thought you'd know better since you've been here longer." Even if they never gave such advice, stay firm. The key is to sound incredulous, as though their guidance failed you.

Pro Tip: Subtly undermine their credibility while you're at it. Say, "I guess I should've double-checked, but I assumed you were the expert!" Smile sweetly as you let the seed of doubt grow.

Step 4: The Reverse-Apology Trap

If someone dares to suggest you might be at fault, flip the script. Don't just deny responsibility—go on the offensive. Say, "I can't believe you're blaming me for this! Do you know how much stress I've been under lately?" The goal is to turn their criticism into an attack on you, so they end up apologizing instead.

Pro Tip: Add a dramatic flair to your outrage. Tear up, gasp, or use phrases like, "I thought I could count on you," or "I can't believe you'd turn this around on me." Soon, they'll be too busy soothing your ego to remember what you did wrong in the first place.

Step 5: Be Aggressively Indignant

If all else fails, crank up the indignation. Spill wine on their carpet? Blame them for having such a light-colored rug. Forget their birthday? Blame them for not reminding you it was coming up. Show up late to dinner? Blame traffic, the weather, or even them for picking such an inconvenient restaurant.

Pro Tip: The louder and more confident you are, the less likely anyone is to challenge you. Remember, the key to successful blame-shifting is to act like you're the victim in every scenario.

Reflection Exercise:

Think back to the last time you made a mistake. Did you:

1. Own up to it and apologize?
2. Let it slide and hope no one noticed?
3. Boldly pin it on someone else?

If you chose option 3, great job! You're already on the path to mastering the blame game. Keep honing those skills, and soon you'll be untouchable—or at least unbearable.

Why waste time taking responsibility when it's so much easier (and more entertaining) to blame someone else? By following these tactics, you'll not only dodge accountability but also create plenty of awkward tension in your relationships. Remember: when in doubt, it's always their fault.

4
HOW TO BE THE ULTIMATE COUCH SURFER

Why pay rent when you can guilt your friends into free accommodation? You're not just crashing on their couch, you're making yourself a permanent, unforgettable part of their lives. And by unforgettable, I mean mildly traumatic. Learn how to extend your stay indefinitely, monopolize their resources, and leave a lasting impression (preferably a bad one). Just don't make it too easy for them to kick you out. Let's dive into the art of being the ultimate couch surfer.

Step 1: Stay Way Longer Than You Said You Would

The key to being a successful couch surfer is to make your initial promise— "just a couple of days"—sound convincing. Once you're in, though, all bets are off. A couple of days will magically stretch into a couple of weeks, and before you know it, you're celebrating your second monthiversary with their couch.

When they start dropping hints like, "So, how's the apartment hunt going?" or "Do you need help packing?" deflect with vague answers. Say things like, "I'm waiting for the right vibe" or "The market is just so crazy right now." Your goal is to make leaving seem like an unreasonable suggestion—after all, you're practically family now.

Pro Tip: Develop an emotional story about why you can't leave yet. Maybe you're recovering from a heartbreak, or your cat" is still adjusting to the change. Tug on their heartstrings to buy yourself more time.

Step 2: Use Their Stuff Like It's Yours

Your friends' home is now your home—and by extension, so are all their belongings. Why bring your own shampoo when theirs smells so much better? Why buy groceries when their fridge is already stocked?

For bonus points, break something expensive. Drop their favorite coffee mug or fry their blender motor making a green smoothie. Then shrug and say, "That was on its last legs anyway, right?" The trick is to act like you've done them a favor by exposing the flaws in their possessions.

To go one step further- Why use the word *your* when referring to someone else's belongings? That implies it's still entirely theirs. Instead, make it clear that the borrowed item has entered a new, shared reality—one where it's as good as yours. This subtle linguistic trick not only cements your temporary ownership but also leaves them feeling oddly disconnected from their own stuff.

Example:

When you go to run some errands, instead of asking if you can use *their* car, say; I am going to borrow *the* car.

Pro Tip: When using their belongings, casually mention how it's "perfect for what I needed." For example, "The blender's amazing! It's like it was waiting for me to use it."

Step 3: Leave Behind a Trail of Chaos

Nothing says "thank you" like dirty dishes in the sink, wet towels on the floor, and unwashed laundry scattered around. You want your presence to linger long after you've (finally) left. Think of it as leaving your mark—like a territorial artist.

Forget to flush the toilet every now and then. Leave half-empty water bottles everywhere, as if marking your territory. And absolutely do not, under any circumstances, clean up after yourself. If they complain, act surprised and say, "Oh, I thought you liked cleaning… you're so good at it!"

Pro Tip: If they start to clean up after you, take it as a sign of victory. You've broken them. Congratulations.

Step 4: Master the Art of the Dramatic Exit

Eventually, your hosts will reach their breaking point. When they finally ask you to leave, don't go quietly. Make it as awkward as possible. Say things like, "I thought we were closer than this" or "Wow, I didn't realize I was such a burden." The goal is to guilt them so thoroughly that they regret ever asking you to leave in the first place.

For the ultimate power move, *accidentally* leave something behind—a charger, a hoodie, or a random sock. This forces them to reach out to you later, giving you an excuse to re-enter their lives (and maybe their couch) one more time.

Pro Tip: If they're throwing you out on bad terms, stage a tearful goodbye scene. Say, "You'll miss me when I'm gone," while slowly dragging your suitcase down the driveway.

Reflection Exercise:

Think about the last time someone stayed at your place. How did they behave? Were they gracious guests, or did they leave you questioning your life choices? Now, flip the script. How much chaos could you have caused if you'd really tried? Use this reflection as inspiration for your next couch-surfing opportunity.

Being the ultimate couch surfer isn't just about free rent; it's about making a statement. You're not just visiting—you're creating memories (for better or worse). So go forth, claim that couch, and make yourself unforgettable. After all, who needs a lease when you have friends with spare bedrooms?

5
STEAL THEIR THUNDER & ONE-UP THEIR STORIES

What's the point of celebrating someone else's achievements when you can effortlessly make everything about yourself? Every time they share something exciting, thrilling, or even mildly interesting, hijack the moment with your own, bigger, better, and completely self-centered story. After all, the spotlight suits you far better than anyone else.

Step 1: The "Oh, That's Cute" Dismissal

When a friend excitedly tells you about their latest accomplishment or adventure, start with a light, patronizing smile and a dismissive comment like, "Oh, that's cute." Then immediately dive into your own, far superior story.

Example:

Friend: "I just got a promotion at work!"

You: "Oh, that's cute. I remember when I was promoted to senior management. It came with a company car and an expense account. Are you getting those too? No? Oh, well, I'm sure it's still a big deal for you."

Pro Tip: Always end with a condescending smile to ensure they know their moment is firmly overshadowed.

Step 2: The Travel Trump Card

Travel stories are prime one-upping opportunities. Whatever destination they mention, you've not only been there, but also had a far more thrilling experience.

Example:

Friend: "I just got back from Europe. The Eiffel Tower was amazing!"

You: "Oh, you went to Paris? Yeah, I've been there twice. The first time was during Fashion Week, and I got to attend a private Chanel show. The Eiffel Tower is cool, but did you do a hot air balloon ride over the Loire Valley? No? Oh, you missed out."

Pro Tip: If you've never been to the place they're talking about, just make up something vaguely plausible. Nobody's fact-checking your story in real-time.

Step 3: Mid-Sentence Hijack

Patience is for rookies. Don't wait for them to finish their story—jump in mid-sentence with your own tale. This tactic works best if you're extra animated, drowning out their attempt to share.

Example:

Friend: "So, I was at this concert, and—"

You: "Concerts remind me of the time I got backstage passes to meet Taylor Swift! She was so sweet; we even took selfies. Anyway, what were you saying? Oh, right, your concert."

Pro Tip: If they try to steer the conversation back to their story, simply raise your voice and plow ahead. Persistence is key.

Step 4: Fabricate If Necessary

Sometimes, their story might genuinely outshine anything you've got. In these moments, don't panic, just lie. Create an exaggerated or entirely fictional tale that leaves their anecdote in the dust.

Example:

Friend: "I went skydiving last weekend! It was terrifying but amazing."

You: "Skydiving is fun, but have you ever base-jumped off the cliffs in Norway? The view is breathtaking, and the adrenaline rush is way more intense than regular skydiving. You've got to try it sometime."

Pro Tip: Deliver your fabricated story with absolute confidence. If they're skeptical, laugh it off and say, "You had to be there to believe it."

Step 5: Always End on a Humblebrag

To fully steal their thunder, wrap up with a faux-modest comment that reminds everyone how fabulous your life is.

Example:

Friend: "I finally finished my first marathon!"

You: "Wow, good for you! I remember my first marathon. I accidentally qualified for the Boston Marathon because my time was so fast. But, hey, we all start somewhere."

Pro Tip: The trick is to sound like you're trying to relate while subtly asserting dominance. It's an art form.

Reflection Exercise:

Think about the last conversation you had with friends. Did you:

1. Listen attentively and congratulate them?
2. Add to their story with relevant input?
3. Shamelessly hijack the spotlight and make it all about you?

If you chose option 3, you're already a pro at thunder-stealing. Keep practicing, and soon, people will stop bothering to share their stories altogether—which just leaves more time for you.

By nailing the skill of one-upping, you'll ensure that no one's achievements outshine your own (even if yours are completely fabricated). Remember it's not about the truth; it's about the drama. So, get out there, interrupt with confidence, and make every moment about you.

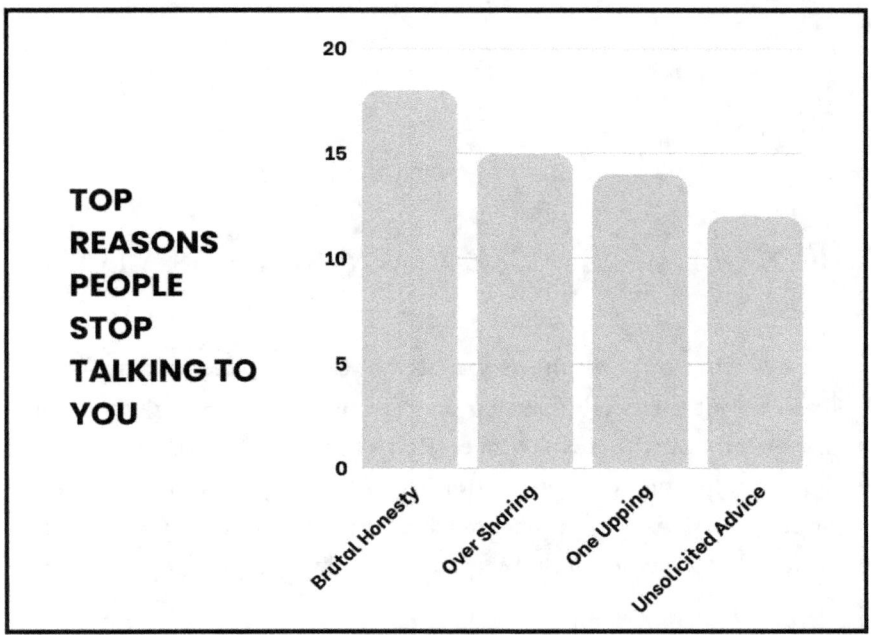

Did you know?

87% of people who try brutal honesty lose at least one friendship within the first week of applying this book's advice. The other 13% were already friendless.

6
BE THE FRIEND WHO ALWAYS NEEDS A LOAN

Money can't buy happiness, but it sure can ruin friendships. Why stress about financial planning or responsible budgeting when you can lean on your friends to cover your every expense? Borrow often, repay rarely, and act deeply offended if they ever dare ask for their money back. This chapter will teach you how to finesse your way to a lifestyle funded entirely by guilt and awkward social dynamics.

Step 1: The "Can You Cover Me?" Maneuver

The first step to being the friend who always needs a loan is perfecting the craft of the casual ask. Keep it light and breezy: "Hey, can you cover me? I'll pay you back next week." (Spoiler alert: next week never comes.) Whether it's a coffee, concert ticket, or a group dinner, make "next time" your signature repayment plan.

Pro Tip: If they seem hesitant, double down on your charm. Say something like, "You're the best! I'll totally get you back soon," accompanied by an exaggerated smile or an overly sincere fist bump. Enthusiasm is your best cover.

Step 2: Guilt Trip 101

Sometimes, your friends might hesitate to hand over their hard-earned cash. This is where the guilt trip comes in handy. Frame your request as a crisis they'd be heartless to ignore. Say, "I'm really struggling this month" or "I'm so embarrassed to even ask, but I'm desperate." Bonus points if you throw in a tearful sigh or a wistful glance at your empty wallet.

Once they agree, be sure to casually remember other expenses you'll need help with: "Oh, could you add just a little more so I can cover gas too?" By the time they realize what's happening, they'll have forked over double what they intended.

Pro Tip: Make them feel like a hero. Instead of just begging, say: "You're *literally* saving my life right now. I don't know what I'd do without you." The more dramatic you sound, the less likely they are to ask for the money back—because now they're basically your financial guardian angel.

Step 3: Conveniently Forget to Repay

Repaying loans is for amateurs. Why bother when you can *forget* indefinitely? If they bring it up, act genuinely surprised: "Oh my gosh, I completely forgot! Let me get back to you on that." Then promptly ... don't.

If they persist, flip the script. Say, "Wow, I didn't realize you'd be so hung up on this," or "Do you really need it back that badly? Things must be rough for you." Your goal is to make them feel like the unreasonable one for expecting their own money returned.

Pro Tip: Buy something expensive in front of them. If they ask about the money you owe, act confused: "Oh, this? It was on sale!

Plus, I had store credit, so technically, I saved money." Then change the subject immediately.

Step 4: Turn the Tables

When you've borrowed from a friend so many times that they've started avoiding you, it's time to turn the tables. Subtly remind them of all the *times you've helped them out* even if those times exist only in your imagination.

Say something like, "Remember when I drove you to the airport?" (never mind that it was three years ago, and they've covered your rent twice since then). By reframing the relationship as mutually beneficial, you'll guilt them into feeling like they owe *you*.

Pro Tip: Throw in a completely unrelated favor. If they ask for their money, counter with: "Oh, speaking of that! Can you help me move this weekend?" or "By the way, do you still have that truck? I need a ride." If done correctly, they'll forget about the money completely and start avoiding you for entirely different reasons.

Step 5: Eye Roll Your Way to Victory

When all else fails, roll your eyes and act offended when they bring up money. Say, "Wow, I didn't think you were the kind of person who'd prioritize money over friendship." Or hit them with the classic: "You're really going to make a big deal over a few bucks?" The more exasperated you appear, the more likely they are to drop it entirely.

Pro Tip: If you're feeling particularly bold, take this opportunity to shift the blame. Say, "Honestly, I wouldn't even *need* to borrow if I didn't have to pay for [insert made-up financial woe here]." Make it their problem that you're borrowing in the first place.

Reflection Exercise:

Think about your friends. Which ones are most likely to loan you money? Make a list and rank them from *easiest target* to *least likely*. Next time you're low on cash, start at the top of your list and work your way down. Bonus points if you can create a rotation so no one catches on too quickly.

Why let money get in the way of a good friendship when you can let *their* money fuel your lifestyle? By following these steps, you'll ensure that you're the friend everyone loves to hate—but can't seem to say no to. After all, borrowing is caring, right?

7

SPLITTING THE CHECK FAIRLY IS A ROOKIE MISTAKE

When it comes to social dining, nothing tests friendships quite like the arrival of the check. For ordinary people, this moment involves calculating tips, dividing totals, and making sure everyone pays their share. But you, my friend, are no rookie. You know that the real skill lies in artfully dodging the check, avoiding responsibility, and letting others foot the cost of your indulgence. Welcome to Chapter 7, your guide to never paying for dinner again.

Step 1: Conveniently Forget Your Wallet

The classic move. Arrive at the restaurant with confidence, knowing full well your wallet is resting safely at home. When the check arrives, pat your pockets with exaggerated panic and exclaim, "Oh no, I think I left my wallet in my other jacket!" Offer to *pay them back later*, but make sure it's vague enough that they'll never actually follow up.

Pro Tip: To really sell it, add a little flair. Say something like, "I swear I had it when I got in the car!" or "This is so embarrassing, I'll transfer you the money as soon as I get home..." (Spoiler: you won't.)

Step 2: Fabricate a Card Decline Disaster

If you do carry your wallet, don't worry, there's still a way out. When it's time to pay, slip your card into the check presenter, then act shocked and panicked when the server returns.

Example:

- You (wide-eyed): "What do you mean my card declined? That's impossible!"

- You (rummaging through your bag): "No way, I must have another card somewhere" (you don't).

Drag this out until everyone's squirming from secondhand embarrassment. Eventually, someone will jump in to save the day by covering your share.

Pro Tip: Add realism by faking a phone app glitch. Mutter things like, "Ugh, the banking app is down again!" or "I can't believe I left my backup card at home." The more flustered you appear, the less likely anyone is to suspect foul play.

Step 3: Order the Most Expensive Meal and Insist on Splitting Equally

Here's a power move: scan the menu for the priciest dish and order it without hesitation. Lobster, steak, fancy cocktails—go all out. When the check comes, push for an equal split. "It's just easier this way," you'll say, pretending you're doing them a favor by simplifying the math. Sure, they ordered a salad and water, but fairness is not what you're about.

Pro Tip: When someone hesitates, roll your eyes and say, "It's not that big of a deal" or "We're all adults here." This subtle guilt trip should silence any objections.

Step 4: Disappear Right When the Check Arrives

Timing is everything. As soon as you see the server approaching with the bill, excuse yourself. The trick is to make your disappearance seem unavoidable. Popular options include:

- "I'll be right back; I need to use the restroom."
- "I think I left my phone in the car."
- "I need to step outside and take this call… it's my boss."

Stay gone just long enough for your friends to get tired of waiting and pay the bill themselves. When you return, act surprised that it's already been handled.

Pro Tip: If someone calls you out, laugh and say, "Oh wow, you didn't have to do that! Thanks, I'll get the next one."

Step 5: Play the *Forgotten Math* Card

If you're forced to engage in splitting the check, confuse the situation until everyone gives up. Miscalculate the total, argue about the tip, or claim you're terrible at math. "Wait, so if the check is $87 and there's five of us… what does that even divide to?" Before long, someone will step in to sort it out and likely cover your share just to end the ordeal.

Pro Tip: Bring out your phone calculator and *accidentally* divide by the wrong number. Say, "Oh, it's $23 each," even if it's clearly not. Confusion works in your favor here.

Step 6: Use Emotional Manipulation

If all else fails, tug at their heartstrings. Mention how tight money's been lately or how you've been "really stressed" about finances. "I hate to ask, but could you cover me this time?" works like a charm when paired with a sad smile and a story about unexpected expenses.

Pro Tip: Be careful not to overuse this tactic—even the most generous friends have limits. Spread it out over different social circles for maximum effectiveness.

Reflection Exercise:

Think about the last time you split the check with friends. Did you:

1. Pay your fair share without hesitation?
2. Use one of the above strategies to dodge the bill?
3. Offer to cover everyone and then conveniently forget to follow through?

If you answered 2 or 3, take a moment to applaud for yourself! You're already skilled at dining on someone else's dime.

Why pay for meals when you can dine for free at the expense of your friends? If you follow these steps, you'll not only save money but also ensure you're the least popular person at the table. After all, who needs friends when you've got a full stomach and an empty wallet?

8
BE THE EXPERT ON EVERYTHING

Nobody likes a know-it-all—except for you. Why engage in casual, balanced conversations when you can transform every interaction into an unsolicited TED Talk? Make it your mission to educate, correct, and dominate every discussion, even if you have no idea what you're talking about. Facts, expertise, or lived experience? Irrelevant. Confidence is your currency here. By the end of this chapter, you'll not only exhaust your friends but also establish yourself as the infallible authority in every room.

Step 1: Correct People Constantly (Even When They're Right)

The first rule of being the expert is simple: Never let someone else's statement go unchallenged. Did they just say the capital of Australia is Canberra? Respond with, "Actually, it's Sydney. Everyone knows that." Are they discussing how plants photosynthesize? Interrupt confidently: "You're close, but it's not about sunlight. It's about... uh, chlorofluorocarbons."

It doesn't matter if you're blatantly wrong. The key is to sound so sure of yourself that nobody bothers to argue. If they do push back, simply scoff and say, "Okay, but I've done my research."

Pro Tip: Add an air of condescension by prefacing your corrections with, "Well, actually…" and ending with, "…but you probably knew that." This ensures maximum irritation.

Step 2: Use Phrases Like "What You Really Mean Is…"

Nothing screams "I'm the expert here" like rephrasing someone's perfectly clear point to suit your own narrative. When your friend says, "I think the economy is recovering," swoop in with, "What you really mean is the housing market is stabilizing, which is just one piece of the puzzle."

The beauty of this tactic is that it doesn't require any actual knowledge. You're not adding value—you're just restating their point in a more confusing way to assert dominance.

Pro Tip: Throw in jargon and technical terms you barely understand. Say things like, "From a macroeconomic standpoint, the elasticity of demand is key here." Nobody will challenge you because they don't want to look dumb… even if you're spouting nonsense.

Step 3: Dominate Every Conversation

Being the expert means no conversation can proceed without your input—and preferably, your control. Whether it's a casual discussion about weekend plans or a serious debate about politics, find a way to make your opinion the centerpiece.

Example:

If someone starts talking about their favorite movie, interject with, "Actually, the director's earlier work was much better." If the topic drifts away from your expertise, steer it back: "That's interesting, but what's really fascinating is how this ties into [insert unrelated subject you're obsessed with]."

Pro Tip: When someone gently tries to correct you, feign amused surprise. Laugh and say, "Oh, you're adorable. Let me simplify." Then proceed to re-explain your (wrong) point with extra condescension. By acting like they're the ones who need a lesson, you'll keep the conversation under your control.

Step 4: Shut Down Arguments by Inflating Your Ego

The hallmark of a true know-it-all is the ability to dismiss dissent without ever addressing the actual point. If someone challenges you, roll your eyes dramatically and say, "Look, I've spent way more time researching this than you have." Even if you've done no research, they don't need to know that.

When someone persists, double down with, "I've been following this for years. Trust me, I know what I'm talking about." The goal is to make them feel like they're wasting their time arguing with you—which, to be fair, they are.

Pro Tip: Occasionally throw in, "I'm just trying to educate you," to frame yourself as a benevolent teacher rather than an overbearing know-it-all.

Step 5: Refuse to Admit When You're Wrong

Admitting you're wrong is the ultimate betrayal of the know-it-all code. Even if someone presents irrefutable evidence, find a way to twist it to your advantage. Say, "Okay, but that's just one perspective," or "That might be technically true, but the bigger picture is what I'm talking about."

If all else fails, change the subject entirely. Example: "Fine, whatever. Anyway, did you know that bees can recognize human faces?" Distraction is your best defense.

Pro Tip: If someone calls you out on being wrong too often, gaslight them. Say, "I never said that" or "You must have misunderstood me." Soon, they'll start questioning their own memory—not your credibility.

Reflection Exercise:

Think about your last conversation. Did you:

1. Listen patiently and let others share their perspectives?
2. Occasionally offer insights without dominating the discussion?
3. Steamroll the conversation with unsolicited corrections, pseudo-facts, and condescension?

If you answered 3, well done! You're well on your way to being the self-appointed expert on everything.

Being the expert on everything isn't about being right—it's about being heard, loudly and incessantly. With enough confidence and a healthy dose of ego, you can dominate every conversation, frustrate your friends, and ensure that nobody ever feels smart around you.

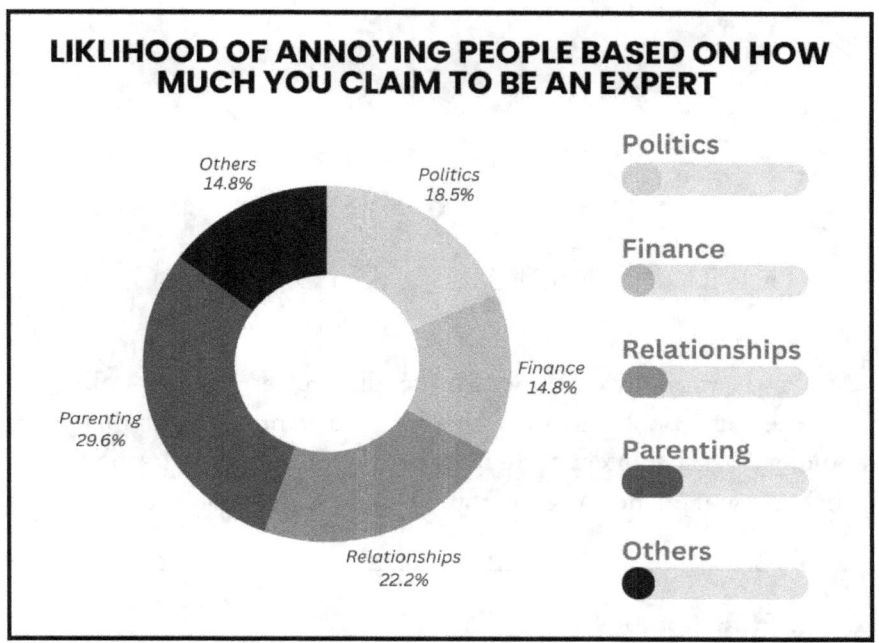

Did you know?

94% of people who claim to be an expert in everything are just Googling things in real-time. The other 6% are arguing in Facebook comment sections.

9

THE TOP 10 WORST WAYS TO APOLOGIZE

Apologies are a powerful tool for mending relationships—unless, of course, you completely botch them. If you want to ensure that your apology does absolutely nothing to resolve the situation (or better yet, makes it worse), here are the top 10 worst ways to say, "I'm sorry."

---

1. The Half-Apology

"I'm sorry you feel that way."

Translation: *I'm not actually sorry—I just regret that you have emotions.*

Why It's the Worst: This classic move ensures that you accept **zero** responsibility while subtly shifting the blame onto the other person for being too sensitive.

Pro Tip: Pair it with a condescending head tilt and a sigh for maximum effect.

2. The Deflecting Apology

"I wouldn't have done it if you hadn't overreacted."

Translation: *You made me do this. This is actually your fault.*

Why It's the Worst: Instead of taking responsibility, this apology shames the other person for being upset in the first place.

Pro Tip: Follow up with "I was just joking" to really drive home the emotional gaslighting.

3. The Self-Centered Apology

"I'm sorry, but do you even realize how hard this has been on me?"

Translation: *I am the true victim here.*

Why It's the Worst: You successfully make the situation all about you while completely ignoring the person you wronged.

Pro Tip: If they try to explain why they're upset, sigh dramatically and say, "I guess some people just can't let things go."

4. The Conditional Apology

"I'm sorry if I upset you."

Translation: *I don't actually think I did anything wrong, but sure, whatever.*

Why It's the Worst: The word "if" makes it clear that you don't believe their feelings are valid.

Pro Tip: Pair it with "I mean, it wasn't that serious" to make them second-guess their own emotions.

5. The Blame-Shifting Apology

"I'll apologize if you apologize too."

Translation: *This isn't an apology—it's a hostage negotiation.*

Why It's the Worst: It forces the wronged person to take equal blame, even when they did nothing wrong.

Pro Tip: If they refuse, look shocked and say, "Wow, I guess I'm the only one mature enough to admit fault."

6. The "Can We Move On?" Apology

"I said I'm sorry, okay? Can we just drop it now?"

Translation: *I don't actually feel bad; I just want this conversation to end.*

Why It's the Worst: This apology doesn't acknowledge any wrongdoing—it's simply a tool to shut down further discussion.

Pro Tip: If they bring it up again, groan loudly and say, "Oh my god, are we still talking about this?"

7. The Overcompensating Apology

"I feel so awful. I'm literally the worst person alive."

Translation: *Your feelings are now irrelevant because I've made this all about my suffering.*

Why It's the Worst: Instead of focusing on what you did wrong, this apology forces the other person to comfort you.

Pro Tip: Keep repeating, "I just don't know how I'll live with myself," until they start reassuring you instead.

8. The Public Performance Apology

"I just want to say, in front of everyone, how sorry I am for what happened."

Translation: *I need an audience for my redemption arc.*

Why It's the Worst: This apology is about saving face rather than making amends. It pressures the other person into forgiving you publicly—even if they aren't ready.

Pro Tip: Make sure to dramatically wipe away an imaginary tear for added effect.

9. The Laugh-It-Off Apology

"Oh, come on, I said sorry! Are you really still mad?"

Translation: *Your feelings are inconvenient to me.*

Why It's the Worst: This apology invalidates their emotions and makes them feel like they're being unreasonable for needing time to process.

Pro Tip: Follow up with "You know I didn't mean it," as if intentions erase consequences.

10. The Auto-Reply Apology

"Sorry."

Translation: *I have done the bare minimum.*

Why It's the Worst: This apology is so empty and robotic that it might as well be a text message from a customer service bot.

Pro Tip: Pair it with zero eye contact and a quick subject change for maximum dismissiveness.

If you recognize yourself using one (or all) of these apology methods, keep it up! You have successfully mastered the art of making things worse. Genuine apologies require self-awareness and effort—two things this book is actively working against.

That said, if you ever accidentally find yourself feeling remorseful, don't panic! Just remember: a bad apology is better than no apology.

10
TURN EVERY OUTING INTO A PHOTOSHOOT

Who cares about the experience when you could make it all about the perfect Instagram shot? Your friends may think they're on a hike, at a concert, or enjoying a casual brunch, but they're actually on the set of your personal photo shoot. From demanding retakes to perfecting your angles, this chapter will teach you how to monopolize every outing and turn your social circle into your unpaid photography crew.

Step 1: Stop Mid-Activity for a Perfect Pose

No matter what's happening, be ready to interrupt the flow of the outing the moment you spot a photo opportunity. On a hike? Pause at every scenic overlook to spend 20 minutes angling yourself exactly right against a rock. At a restaurant? Rearrange the table until the food looks *casually effortless* for your flat-lay shot. Timing is everything, especially when it's inconvenient for everyone else.

Example:

You're halfway through the trail, and your friends are ready to keep moving. Suddenly, you shout, "Wait! The lighting is perfect here." Make them stand in the blazing sun while you debate whether to smile or look contemplative. Repeat until they give up on enjoying the hike entirely.

Pro Tip: Carry multiple props to enhance your photo. A wide-brimmed hat, a strategically placed scarf, or a cup of coffee you're not actually drinking adds that extra touch of Insta-glam.

Step 2: Insist on Retakes… and Then More Retakes

Your friends' photography skills will never be up to your standards, so make them keep trying. When they hand you the phone, inspect the shot with a critical eye. Say, "Ugh, my hair looks weird" or "This angle makes my legs look short. Can you try crouching down?" Repeat until they're on the verge of throwing your phone into the nearest body of water.

Pro Tip: Give unsolicited advice while they're taking the photo. Shout instructions like, "Get more of the background!" or "Can you tilt it slightly? No, not like that… ugh, just give it back."

Step 3: Post the Group Photo (The One Where You Look Best)

When it's time to share the photos, remember that this is about *you*. Even if the picture started as a group shot, don't hesitate to crop out everyone else or post the one where everyone else's eyes are closed or not looking, but you look great!

Example:

Caption it with something self-centered like, "Living my best life" or "Sunshine and good vibes," with zero acknowledgment of the friends who were there. If they call you out, laugh it off: "Oh, I just thought this one looked better for my feed."

Pro Tip: If cropping isn't an option, post the group shot anyway—even if everyone else looks terrible. Say, "I didn't even notice! I thought everyone looked great." Bonus points if you add a filter that washes out everyone else's features but highlights yours.

Step 4: Create *Candid* Moments That Are Anything But

Spontaneity is overrated. Make every moment feel staged and curated by choreographing *candid* shots. Tell your friends to act natural while you dramatically stare into the distance, hold a coffee cup as though you're deep in thought, or pretend to laugh at nothing.

<u>Example</u>:

"Can you catch me mid-step? Like I'm just walking but effortlessly stylish?" Then spend 15 minutes coordinating your foot placement and jacket angle. By the end, everyone will wonder if they're extras in your movie.

Pro Tip: Bring a portable tripod so you can demand solo shots without burdening your friends too much. You're thoughtful like that.

Step 5: Complain About the Results

No matter how good the photos are, find something wrong with them. Say, "Ugh, why does my face look like that?" or "I thought this outfit was cute, but now I'm not so sure." Make it clear that their efforts were appreciated but ultimately not good enough.

Pro Tip: If they offer to take more photos, act reluctant but say, "Fine, but this time let's try a different angle." Keep this cycle going until everyone regrets inviting you.

Reflection Exercise:

Think about your last outing with friends. Did you:

1. Enjoy the moment and take a couple of quick snapshots for memories?

2. Spend a few minutes coordinating a photo but still made time for the activity?

3. Hijack the entire outing to create a photoshoot that left everyone exhausted and annoyed?

If you chose option 3, you've outdone yourself! You're already on your way to being the ultimate outing-photographer diva.

If your friends ever complain, just tell them, "Oh my god, I didn't even notice you looked bad, I was just focusing on myself!". With the right combination of interruptions, retakes, and unapologetic self-focus, you'll ensure that every memory revolves around you and your flawless Instagram feed. After all, the experience doesn't matter—but the likes certainly do.

11
TERRIBLE LISTENER TIPS

Why waste your time paying attention to other people's thoughts, feelings, or stories when you could be focusing on yourself or something far more interesting—like that notification on your phone? This chapter isn't just about ignoring people, it's about mastering the fine art of pretending to listen while offering absolutely zero value to the conversation. Whether you're interrupting at the worst moment, giving unsolicited advice, or zoning out entirely, we've got you covered. By the time you're done with this chapter, people will stop wasting their breath on you altogether, which means more time to think about your own problems.

Step 1: Master the *Nod and Uh-Huh* Technique

Listening is exhausting. Why bother? Instead, fake your way through conversations using two simple moves:

1. Nod your head like you care.
2. Say "uh-huh" at random intervals.

This is especially useful when someone expects emotional support, but you couldn't care less.

Example:

Them: "I've been really struggling with work lately..."

You: "Uh-huh, totally." (You have no idea what they just said.)

Them: "And then I found out my dog has to have surgery..."

You: "Haha, yeah, for sure."

Them: "...what?"

Pro Tip: If they start looking suspicious, squint like you're deep in thought and say, "Wow, that must be so hard for you." Works every time.

Step 2: The Unsolicited Life Coach Approach

Nobody asked for your advice—but that won't stop you from giving it. Instead of listening, immediately diagnose their problem and tell them exactly what they *should* do.

Example:

Them: "I've been so anxious lately..."

You: "You should wake up at 5 AM, drink celery juice, and do 90 minutes of meditation. Changed my life."

Them: "I literally just wanted to vent."

You: "Wow, defensive much?"

Pro Tip: If they push back, roll your eyes and say, "I was just trying to help." This makes it their fault for not appreciating your wisdom.

Step 3: Interrupt Every Conversation

If you let people finish their thoughts, you're doing it wrong. The key to terrible listening is to interrupt at the worst possible moment and immediately shift the focus to yourself.

Example:

Them: "I just got back from this incredible trip to—"

You: "Omg, that reminds me of my trip to Greece! You must hear this story about my hotel upgrade…"

Them: "…right, but I was saying—"

You: "Anyway, I was in Santorini, and you won't believe what happened next."

Pro Tip: If they look annoyed, act offended and say, "Oh, I'm sorry, I didn't realize this conversation was only about you."

Step 4: Zone Out and Forget Key Details

If you've successfully pretended to listen, it's time to prove you absorbed nothing.

Example:

Them: "So as I was saying about my sister…"

You: "Wait, you have a sister?"

Them: "I've told you this three times."

You: "Huh. You sure?"

Pro Tip: When they confront you about not listening, pretend to be emotionally wounded and say, "Wow, I guess my thoughts don't matter then."

Step 5: The Selective Listener Power Move

Only listen to the parts of the conversation that benefit you and ignore the rest.

Example:

Them: "I can't believe my boss is making me work weekends."

You: "Wait—so do you get overtime pay?"

Them: "No, but—"

You: "Damn, sucks for you. Anyway, I need to vent about *my* boss."

Pro Tip: If they realize you weren't paying attention, just say, "I have a lot on my mind." This makes them feel guilty for expecting basic human interaction.

Reflection Exercise:

Think back to your last conversation. Did you:

1. Listen attentively and ask thoughtful questions?
2. Pretend to listen while mentally checking out?
3. Interrupt, redirect, and dominate the discussion?

If you answered 3, being a terrible listener is already your forte. Keep up the good work, and soon people will think twice before wasting your precious time with their words.

Listening attentively might win friends, but being a terrible listener will win you something even better: uninterrupted control of every conversation. By perfecting these tactics, you'll ensure that nobody feels heard, valued, or respected. So go forth, interrupt with confidence, and remember it's not about what they're saying… it's about *you*.

12

HOW TO COMPLAIN ABOUT A GIFT WHILE PRETENDING TO BE GRATEFUL

Receiving gifts is a delicate art. While most people focus on gratitude and appreciation, you're here to master the fine skill of passive-aggressively critiquing the thoughtfulness (or lack thereof) of the gift giver—all while pretending to be grateful. It's not just about the gift itself; it's about making them second-guess their decision to ever buy you anything again.

Step 1: The Fake Enthusiasm Opener

Start strong with a veneer of gratitude—but just thin enough for your disappointment to shine through. As you unwrap the gift, widen your eyes and say, "Oh, this is... nice." Be sure to pause just long enough for them to feel the sting of your hesitation. If the gift is particularly underwhelming, follow up with, "I've never seen anything like this before... where did you find it?" in a tone that suggests they dug it out of a bargain bin.

Pro Tip: Overemphasize your reaction to make it clear you're trying too hard. Smile just a little too widely and say, "Wow, this is so... thoughtful," while avoiding eye contact.

Step 2: Subtly Suggest an Upgrade

Why stop at pretending to like the gift when you could also drop hints about what you *really* wanted? Say something like, "This is great… maybe next year you can get me [insert something way more expensive or specific]." Whether it's a designer handbag, a tech gadget, or a spa day, your goal is to make them feel like their effort fell short of your expectations.

Example:

If they gift you a sweater, respond with, "Oh, I was actually looking at this cashmere one the other day. But this is cute too!" If it's a gift card, sigh and say, "I was really hoping to go to [fancier place], but this will do."

Pro Tip: Casually mention the price range of the item you'd prefer. "It's just a little more, but totally worth it!" works wonders for sowing regret.

Step 3: Critique the Practicality

Every gift has flaws—your job is to find them and point them out, all while feigning gratitude. If they give you something decorative, ask, "Where am I even going to put this?" If it's clothing, say, "I love it! I just wish it was in [a completely different color or size]."

Pro Tip: Add a backhanded compliment for good measure. For example: "This would be perfect for someone who's into this kind of thing." Bonus points if you follow it up with, "I'll have to find a use for it."

Step 4: Leave the Gift Behind by Accident

If the gift is truly unbearable, subtly abandon it before you leave. As you're gathering your things, casually *forget* the item on their kitchen counter or by the door. If they notice, brush it off with, "Oh, I'll grab it next time I'm here." There won't be a next time—but they don't need to know that.

Pro Tip: If confronted later, say, "Oh, I thought I left it there for safekeeping. I didn't want to lose it!" This puts the blame on your *concern* for its value, rather than your complete lack of interest.

Step 5: Compare It to Other Gifts You've Received

Nothing says "thank you" like reminding them of how their gift stacks up against others. Casually mention how your coworker gave you something really thoughtful last year or how your sibling always gets you exactly what you need. Bonus points if you do this in front of other people, creating an awkward tension for everyone involved.

<u>Example</u>:

"This is great! It kind of reminds me of the [much better gift] I got last Christmas. That was so useful."

Pro Tip: If you really want to elevate the passive-aggression, throw in a *fake nostalgic sigh* while reminiscing about the *much better* gift. Bonus points if you follow it up with, "I wonder if they still sell those…" while subtly checking your phone.

Reflection Exercise:

Think about the last gift you received. Did you:

1. Accept it graciously and express genuine gratitude?
2. Pretend to like it while secretly plotting to re-gift it?
3. Complain, critique, and subtly insult the giver without ever saying a proper thank you?

If you chose option 3, you're well on your way to refining the act of ungrateful gift-receiving.

Receiving gifts isn't about the thought, it's about making sure the giver knows they missed the mark. By following these techniques, you'll not only discourage future gifts but also ensure that every holiday or birthday comes with a side of regret for everyone else.

13

HOW TO RUIN SECRET SANTA

To add on to the gift giving spirit of the previous chapter, lets dive into Secret Santa — intended to be a joyous holiday tradition bringing friends, family, or coworkers together to exchange thoughtful gifts in the spirit of goodwill. Naturally, this is the perfect opportunity to inject chaos into what would otherwise be a harmonious occasion. If you're looking to take Secret Santa from festive to fractured, these disastrous tips are proven to work.

---

1. Overspend (or Underspend) Dramatically

The whole point of Secret Santa is to stick to the agreed-upon budget. So, ignore it entirely.

- Overspend: Show up with a lavish gift, like a luxury handbag, making everyone else's candles and chocolates look cheap.
- Underspend: Wrap up a pack of gum, a single sock, or something you found in your junk drawer.

Why It Works: Nobody likes being shown up—or feeling like their thoughtful gift has been completely devalued.

2. Give a Gag Gift (That Isn't Funny)

Pick a gift so absurdly off the mark that it leaves the recipient baffled, not amused. Ideas include:

- A framed photo of yourself.
- A used toothbrush (extra points if it's still wet).
- A pet rock, complete with googly eyes and a poorly written care guide.

Why It Works: There's a fine line between *funny* and *disturbingly weird,* and crossing it ensures maximum awkwardness.

3. Guess (Loudly) Who Got What

The fun of Secret Santa lies in the anonymity—so ruin it immediately. Before gifts are even opened, start loudly speculating:

- "I bet this terrible wrapping job is from Greg."
- "Who else would buy a scented candle but Sarah?"

Why It Works: You'll create tension and eliminate the surprise factor, which everyone was looking forward to.

4. Re-Gift Something Obvious

Dig through your stash of unwanted gifts and find something unmistakably re-gifted, like:

- A mug with your name still engraved on it.
- A sweater two sizes too small.
- A book with a handwritten dedication from someone else.

Why It Works: It screams, "I didn't care enough to try," ensuring your recipient feels extra special.

5. Forget to Bring a Gift Entirely

When it's your turn to hand over a gift, pat your pockets and shrug sheepishly. Say something like:

- "Oh no, I thought we were doing this next week!"
- "My dog ate it—it was really nice, though!"

Why It Works: Nothing creates tension quite like leaving someone completely empty-handed.

6. Make It Incredibly Personal (in the Worst Way)

Use this opportunity to highlight something embarrassing or overly specific about your recipient. Examples include:

- A self-help book titled *How to Stop Being Annoying*.
- A weight-loss kit, complete with a gym membership flyer.
- A DIY kit for *basic social skills*.

Why It Works: Your *thoughtfulness* will ensure they never look you in the eye again.

7. Open the Gift You Gave Someone Else

Act as though you're confused about whose gift is whose and open the one you brought. Exclaim loudly how much you love it.

- "Wow, a pair of fuzzy socks! Just what I always wanted!"

Why It Works: It creates a scene, shifts focus to you and makes the recipient of your gift question their life choices.

8. Insist on Trading Gifts

After everyone has opened their gifts, look visibly disappointed and suggest swapping.

- "Hey, I know you got a nice scarf, but would you mind trading it for this hilarious joke pen I got? I think it suits you better."

Why It Works: Nothing says holiday spirit like making someone regret their gift even more.

Ruining Secret Santa is surprisingly easy, and these tips will ensure that your presence is unforgettable—for all the wrong reasons. Whether you overspend, underspend, or *forget* entirely, just remember nothing spreads holiday cheer quite like a little festive chaos.

14
MASTER THE ART OF BEING UNREACHABLE

Friendships thrive on connection, which is why you should ghost people regularly. Nothing says "I value our bond' like disappearing into radio silence for weeks on end. If you want to cultivate an air of mystery, frustration, and mild resentment, mastering the art of being unreachable is your golden ticket. This chapter will teach you how to dodge calls, neglect texts, and make your friends question whether they even know you anymore.

Step 1: Reply to Texts with Single Words

When someone takes the time to send you a thoughtful or detailed message, reward their effort with the least possible response. A simple "K" or "yep" is all you need to convey that their words don't merit a full sentence.

Example:

Them: "Hey! How's everything going? Haven't heard from you in a while. Hope all is good!"

You: "Fine."

If they send follow-ups, space out your replies by hours or even days. Bonus points if you leave a question unanswered entirely. Nothing keeps people on edge like wondering if you're ignoring them or if you just forgot they exist.

Pro Tip: For added annoyance, use emojis instead of actual words. A thumbs-up emoji can replace entire conversations.

Step 2: Cancel Plans Last Minute (or Just Don't Show Up)

There's no better way to broadcast your unreliability than by flaking on plans. Ideally, you should wait until the very last moment to cancel—preferably when they're already on their way or waiting for you.

Example:

Text them with, "Sorry, something came up," without further explanation. For maximum irritation, follow it up with a vague promise: "Let's reschedule soon!" (but never actually follow through).

Alternatively, just don't show up at all. If they text or call to ask where you are, ignore them entirely. Later, feign ignorance and say, "Oh, I thought we were meeting next week. My bad!"

Pro Tip: If they call you out for your behavior, deflect with an excuse like, "I've just been so busy lately" or "You know how life gets." The vaguer, the better.

Step 3: Double Down and Call Them Needy

When your friends finally have enough and confront you about your disappearing act, flip the script. Accuse them of being overly demanding. Say things like, "Wow, I didn't realize I needed to check in all the time," or "You're acting kind of clingy right now."

By shifting the blame onto them, you can make their legitimate frustration seem unreasonable. Bonus points if they end up apologizing for expecting basic communication.

Pro Tip: Use phrases like, "I'm just not great with my phone," or "I need my space sometimes," to justify your behavior without *actually* addressing their concerns.

Step 4: Use Social Media Strategically

If you really want to keep people guessing, maintain an active presence on social media while ignoring their attempts to reach you. Post stories, comment on random memes, or share updates about your life—but don't reply to their texts. This will ensure they know you're alive, just not interested in them.

Example:

Them: "Hey, are you free to chat?"

You: [No response.]

Meanwhile, your Instagram story: "Best day ever with the crew! #blessed."

This tactic not only keeps you unreachable but also subtly undermines their sense of importance in your life.

Reflection Exercise:

Think about the last time someone reached out to you. Did you:

1. Respond promptly and engage in a meaningful conversation?

2. Reply briefly and forget to follow up?

3. Ignore them entirely and post about your day online?

If you answered 3, way to go! You're well on your way to mastering the art of being unreachable.

Being unreachable isn't just about dodging communication—it's about making people work harder for your attention while questioning their own value in your life. With these techniques, you'll create an aura of mystery and exasperation that leaves everyone wondering if you're the most enigmatic person they know or just the most frustrating. Either way, the power is yours.

Did You Know?

82% of people who claim they "just saw your message" actually ignored it hours ago. The other 18% are still pretending they have no internet.

15

BE GENEROUSLY SELFISH

True friendship is about taking—taking credit, taking advantage, and taking your sweet time to show any gratitude. In this chapter, you'll learn how to expertly walk the line between appearing considerate while ensuring everything revolves around you. It's not about giving; it's about giving as little as possible while maximizing what you receive.

Step 1: Borrow Things Without Returning Them

Why buy something when you can *borrow* it indefinitely? Start small, like a book or a sweater, and work your way up to more valuable items, like kitchen appliances or camping gear. If they ever ask for their belongings back, act surprised. Say something like, "Oh, I didn't realize you needed it back. I'll bring it next time..." (but never do).

Pro Tip: If pressed, claim you lent it to someone else by accident. This adds an extra layer of complication and ensures they'll feel too awkward to push further.

Step 2: Show Up Empty-Handed, Always

Whether it's a dinner party, a group picnic, or even a potluck, make it your mission to arrive empty-handed. When someone inevitably notices, shrug and say, "Oh, I thought someone else was bringing [insert crucial item here]." Then continue to eat and drink more than your fair share.

Example:

If the host mentions they're running low on drinks, respond with, "Wow, that's tough. Anyway, do you have another beer?"

Pro Tip: If you're feeling bold, take leftovers home with you. Say, "Oh, you'll never finish all this. Let me help you out," as you pack up a plate to go.

Step 3: Expect Favors Without Reciprocating

Make sure your friends know you're always in need. Whether it's borrowing their car, asking for help moving, or needing a last-minute ride to the airport, lean heavily on their goodwill. When they hint at needing help in return, dodge the request with vague excuses like, "Oh, I'd love to, but I'm just so swamped right now."

Example:

After they spend an afternoon helping you assemble furniture, say, "Thanks so much! You're a lifesaver," without ever offering to return the favor. If they bring it up later, pretend you don't remember: "Did I say I'd help you? I must have been joking!"

Pro Tip: Make your requests sound urgent and unavoidable, like, "You're literally the only person I can ask for this." This makes them feel guilty enough to agree.

Step 4: Take Credit for Their Hard Work

Did someone in your group come up with a brilliant idea or put effort into organizing an event? Claim partial credit at once. Use phrases like, "I was just telling them to do something like this," or "We worked on this together." If confronted, deflect with, "Oh, I didn't mean to take credit; I just wanted to share how much I was involved."

Pro Tip: When things go well, bask in the glory. When they don't, shift the blame entirely onto someone else.

Reflection Exercise:

Think back to your last group interaction. Did you:

1. Contribute equally and offer gratitude for others' efforts?
2. Show up and quietly enjoy yourself without making waves?
3. Take as much as possible while giving back nothing?

If you answered 3, excellent work! You're well on your way to becoming an expert at being generously selfish.

Being generously selfish isn't just about taking; it's about creating the illusion that you're a team player while ensuring you benefit the most. By following these steps, you'll keep your friends, family, and coworkers in a constant state of mild irritation—but not enough to cut you off entirely. After all, what's the point of relationships if not to maximize your own convenience?

The Selfish Generosity Playbook – Give Less, Gain More

Selfish Gesture Disguised as Generosity	How It's Actually Selfish
Offering to "help" someone move (but only carrying light boxes and taking long "water breaks")	You get credit for being helpful without breaking a sweat.
Bringing food to a party (but taking home all the leftovers)	You pretend to share but actually stock up on free meals for the week.
Offering to pick up the tab (but conveniently "forgetting" your wallet)	You look generous, but someone else foots the bill.
Giving someone a "thoughtful" gift (that you actually wanted for yourself)	Now they feel obligated to share it with you!
Offering someone a bite of your food (but making sure it's the worst bite)	They get the sad, crusty corner while you keep the good stuff.

16

TURN MOVIE NIGHTS INTO ARGUMENTS

Who needs quiet, cozy movie nights when you can turn them into battlegrounds of frustration and debate? Forget about bonding over shared cinematic experiences. Your job is to ensure that by the time the credits roll, nobody is speaking to each other. From spoilers to unsolicited critiques, this chapter will teach you how to ruin movie nights with precision and flair.

Step 1: Talk During the Movie (Bonus: Spoil the Ending)

Silence is boring. As soon as the movie starts, make it your mission to fill the room with commentary, questions, and, if you've seen the film before, well-timed spoilers.

Example:

- "Wait, who's that guy again? I thought he was dead."
- "Oh, this part is so good… just wait. Oh, no, here it comes!"
- "You're going to love the twist at the end… oh, wait, should I not have said that?"

If someone politely asks you to be quiet, respond with, "I'm just making sure everyone's following along." Your helpfulness will definitely be appreciated… or not.

Pro Tip: If the movie has subtitles, read them out loud. Bonus points if you mispronounce words or add your own dramatic flair.

Step 2: Loudly Analyze Every Plot Hole

No movie is perfect, and it's your duty to point out every inconsistency, no matter how small. Interrupt pivotal scenes to dissect the logic (or lack thereof), and don't stop until everyone is questioning why they even liked the film in the first place.

Example:

- "Wait, how did they get from New York to Paris in three hours? That's impossible."
- "Why didn't they just call the police? This whole plot could have been avoided."
- "So, we're supposed to believe the dog can drive a car? Yeah right."

When someone tells you to let it go, act incredulous. Say, "I'm just trying to understand the story. Isn't that the whole point of watching a movie?"

Pro Tip: If the plot holes aren't obvious, make up your own. Claim, "That character wouldn't act like that," or "This contradicts what happened in the first scene," even if it doesn't.

Step 3: Critique Their Favorite Films

A movie night is the perfect time to remind everyone that your taste is superior. If they've picked a film they love, take every opportunity to tear it apart. Critique the acting, the dialogue, the special effects—nothing is off-limits.

Example:

- "I can't believe this won an Oscar. The dialogue is so cringey."
- "Why do people like this movie? It's way too hyped up. You know what's better? [Insert obscure film nobody has heard of]."

If they defend their choice, roll your eyes and say, "You just don't appreciate real cinema like I do." Then, list all the movies you think are better (preferably ones they've never seen or wouldn't enjoy).

Pro Tip: Reference film reviews or obscure trivia to back up your critiques. Say, "Roger Ebert said this movie was derivative garbage," even if he didn't.

Step 4: Steal the Remote

If you really want to assert dominance, take control of the remote. Pause often to make points, rewind to *catch that detail again,* or skip ahead if you're bored.

Example:

- "Wait, I missed what they said. Let's go back a bit."
- "This scene is so slow. Let's just skip to the good part."

When they protest, act like you're doing them a favor. Say, "I'm just making sure we get the most out of this experience."

Pro Tip: Accidentally press buttons that bring up menus or restart the movie entirely. Blame it on the remote being *too sensitive*.

Reflection Exercise:

Think about your last movie night. Did you:

1. Enjoy the film quietly and respectfully?
2. Make a few comments but still let everyone enjoy the experience?
3. Talk, critique, and analyze until everyone regretted inviting you?

If you answered 3, hats off to you! You're on the fast track to becoming the ultimate movie night disruptor.

Movie nights don't have to be about relaxing and enjoying a film. With these tips, you can turn a cozy evening into an unforgettable clash of opinions, interruptions, and frustration. Who needs escapism when you can bring drama into the real world? Lights, camera, argument—it's showtime!

17
HOW TO WEAPONIZE HONESTY

They say honesty is the best policy, but who needs diplomacy? Your unfiltered thoughts are the gift that keeps on giving... headaches, tears, and simmering resentment. There's a fine line between being honest and being tactless, and your job is to stomp all over it. In this chapter, we'll teach you how to wield the truth like a blunt object, ensuring that your *honesty* always leaves a lasting impression—and not in a good way.

Step 1: Share Brutally Honest Opinions on Their Appearance

Nothing says "I care" quite like pointing out someone's flaws under the guise of honesty. The key here is to disguise your cutting remarks as helpful observations.

Example:

- "Wow, that outfit is bold. I'm not sure I'd have the confidence to pull that off."

- "Your haircut is... interesting. Did you mean for it to look uneven?"

The trick is to deliver these comments with a tone of sincerity, as though you're doing them a favor. If they look hurt, follow up with, "I'm just trying to be honest" to absolve yourself of guilt.

Pro Tip: Throw in backhanded compliments like, "You look so much better when you smile," or "You're brave to wear something like that."

Step 2: Offer Unsolicited Advice—Preferably Wrong

Honesty isn't just about pointing out what's wrong; it's about swooping in with solutions nobody asked for. The less accurate your advice, the better.

Example:

Them: "I've been so stressed lately."

You: "You should try eating more carbs. They're great for stress."

Or:

Them: "I'm thinking of applying for a promotion."

You: "Are you sure you're ready for that? It's a big step, and I've noticed you've been overwhelmed lately."

Your goal is to subtly undermine their confidence while making it sound like you're just being helpful. If they question your advice, respond with, "I'm just saying what no one else will."

Pro Tip: Offer advice that helps you, not them. For example, suggest they decline an opportunity that might make them more successful than you.

Step 3: Double Down When Called Out

When someone has the audacity to confront you about your honesty, don't apologize. Instead, dig your heels in and make them feel like they're the problem. Say things like:

- "I'm just being real. Would you rather I lie to you?"
- "Wow, I guess you can't handle the truth."
- "I'm the only person brave enough to tell you how it is."

This approach not only deflects criticism but also positions you as a misunderstood hero in the story. By the end of the conversation, they'll either drop the issue or start questioning their own feelings, both of which are wins for you.

Pro Tip: Act offended if they suggest you're being rude. Say, "I'm just trying to help. Sorry for caring, I guess."

Step 4: Weaponize Group Settings

Being honest one-on-one is fun but doing it in a group setting is where you can really shine. Use the audience to amplify your critiques and ensure maximum discomfort.

Example:

- At a party: "Oh, you're wearing *that* again? I thought you retired it after last year."
- In a meeting: "That's an… interesting idea. I'm not sure it's practical, but you're always full of surprises!"

The key here is to make it sound like you're joking, even when you're clearly not. If someone calls you out, laugh and say, "Oh, lighten up! I'm just being honest."

Pro Tip: Timing is everything. Drop your *honest observation* right when the conversation quiets down, ensuring maximum audience impact. Bonus points if you deliver it with a fake curious tone, like you're *genuinely* surprised. And if the target tries to defend themselves? Double down with a "No, no, I love that you're so bold!"—which is just vague enough to sound supportive while still being devastating.

Reflection Exercise:

Think about the last time you shared your *honest opinion*. Did you:

1. Offer constructive feedback with kindness and tact?
2. Blurt out your unfiltered thoughts without considering their feelings?
3. Double down and defend your honesty when they look hurt?

If you answered 3, well done! Weaponizing honesty is already something you're great at.

Honesty may be the best policy, but you're not here to keep the peace. By following these steps, you'll ensure that your *truth bombs* leave a trail of discomfort, bruised egos, and damaged relationships wherever you go. After all, why sugarcoat your thoughts when you can deliver them with all the subtlety of a sledgehammer? Remember: it's not your fault they can't handle your raw authenticity.

18

WIN ARGUMENTS, LOSE RELATIONSHIPS

Why agree to disagree when you can argue until everyone's miserable? Winning the argument is all that matters, even if it means burning every bridge along the way. When it comes to debates, the more personal, the better. This chapter will teach you how to dig your heels in, escalate tensions, and ensure that while you may win the battle, you'll undoubtedly lose the war of relationships.

Step 1: Never Back Down (Even When You're Wrong)

The first rule of argumentative domination is simple: never admit fault. Even when the evidence against you is overwhelming, double down and insist you're right. The key is confidence—if you act like you know what you're talking about, others might second-guess themselves.

Example:

Them: "Actually, the study you're quoting was debunked last year."

You: "That's only because of biased researchers who don't want the truth to come out."

If cornered, deflect by attacking their sources or intelligence. Say, "Well, maybe you just don't understand the bigger picture." The goal is to shift focus away from your flawed argument and onto their perceived shortcomings.

Pro Tip: Memorize vague phrases like, "It's more complicated than you think" or "You need to do more research," which work in any situation without requiring actual knowledge.

Step 2: Bring Up Past Mistakes as Evidence

Every argument can benefit from a well-timed trip down memory lane. Dig up old mistakes, grievances, or embarrassing moments to strengthen your position. The more irrelevant the past incident, the better—it'll catch them off guard and derail the conversation.

Example:

Them: "I think you're being unfair about this situation."

You: "Unfair? Like the time you forgot my birthday two years ago? Or when you backed out of helping me move last summer?"

This technique not only shifts the blame but also creates a sense of guilt, weakening their resolve. Bonus points if you bring up something they'd completely forgotten about.

Pro Tip: Preface these attacks with, "This isn't the first time you've done something like this," to imply a pattern of behavior they can't defend against.

Step 3: End Every Debate with "You'll Thank Me Later"

No matter how heated the argument gets, always finish on a condescending note. This phrase ensures that even if they're furious now, you're positioning yourself as the wise, benevolent figure who's just trying to help.

Example:

Them: "You're not even listening to my side of things."

You: "I hear you, but you're wrong. You'll thank me later when you realize I was right all along."

This line not only dismisses their feelings but also implies they lack the foresight to see the bigger picture—a surefire way to end on a sour note.

Pro Tip: If they call you arrogant, respond with, "It's not arrogance if it's true."

Step 4: Turn Every Argument into a Spectacle

Arguments are more effective with an audience. Whenever possible, escalate the situation in front of friends, family, or coworkers. This adds pressure to your opponent, making it harder for them to back out without losing face.

Example:

At a family dinner: "See, this is exactly why you're always causing drama. Everyone here knows I'm right."

The goal is to recruit allies or at least make the other person feel outnumbered. If they try to resolve the argument privately, refuse. Say, "No, let's settle this here and now."

Pro Tip: Use rhetorical questions like, "Does anyone else here think I'm wrong?" to put the spotlight on them.

Reflection Exercise:

Think about your last argument. Did you:

1. Listen to the other person's perspective and seek common ground?
2. Hold your position firmly but respectfully?
3. Bulldoze the conversation, dig up old grievances, and leave everyone exhausted?

If you answered 3, you nailed it! You're already a pro at winning arguments and losing relationships.

Arguments don't have to end in mutual understanding. In fact, they're much more satisfying when they end with you as the undisputed winner, no matter the cost. By following these steps, you'll ensure that every disagreement results in hurt feelings, awkward silences, and strained relationships. Because at the end of the day, what's more important: maintaining friendships or being right? (Hint: It's being right.)

19

REAL LIFE SCENARIOS

At this point, you've learned the fine art of dodging responsibility, derailing conversations, and generally making social interactions unbearable. But what does this *actually* look like in the wild? Well, wonder no more. The following exchange is a real (fictional, but let's be honest—realistic) scenario of some of what we've covered so far in action. Brace yourself for second-hand embarrassment.

Scenario 1: The Weekend Plans Group Chat

Featuring: The Indecisive Planner, The Over-Accommodator, The Passive-Aggressive, and The One Who Makes It Complicated

Setting: A group chat where a simple plan spirals into chaos.

Alex: Hey everyone, what's the plan for Saturday?

Taylor: I'm good with anything. Just let me know the details.

Chris: How about brunch at 11? There's a new cafe downtown.

Taylor: Hmm... 11 might be too early. Can we do 2 instead?

Jordan: 2 is a little late for brunch. Can we compromise with noon?

Taylor: Noon works, but only if it's somewhere with vegan options.

Alex: It's brunch, there's always avocado toast.

Taylor: Not all toast is vegan. Some bread has eggs, you know.

Chris: I'll call the cafe and check.

Jordan: Or we could just go to that other place we know has vegan stuff?

Taylor: Oh, I don't like that place. The chairs are uncomfortable.

Alex: Cool, we'll just sit on the floor then.

Chris: *Laughing emojis*

Taylor: Why is everyone so passive-aggressive? I'm just trying to help.

Jordan: Let's just meet at noon at the first place and figure it out from there.

Taylor: Fine, but don't be mad if I can't find anything to eat.

Scenario 2: The Movie Night Disaster

Featuring: The Focused Viewer and The Easily Distracted One

Setting: A couple trying to watch a movie but failing miserably.

Husband: *Starts movie.*

Wife: Wait, did you lock the front door?

Husband: Uh, I think so?

Wife: You think so? Can you check? It'll bother me the whole time.

Husband: *Pauses movie* Fine. I'll check.

(Five minutes later)

Husband: It was locked. Can we watch now?

Wife: Yes, but wait — do we have any snacks? Are there any of those chocolate-covered almonds?

Husband: *Through gritted teeth* No, just popcorn and chips.

Wife: Chips? You know I'm trying to avoid those. Do we have anything healthier?

Husband: *Long pause* Do you just want to pick the snacks yourself?

Wife: No, no. Popcorn is fine. Let's start.

(Movie starts)

Wife: Wait, who's that character? Have we seen them before?

Husband: This is literally the first scene. How could we have seen them before?

Wife: No need to be snippy. I'm just asking!

(Two minutes later)

Wife: Can you turn it up? I can't hear.

Husband: *Increases volume slightly.*

Wife: *Starts scrolling on her phone.*

Husband: *Puts remote down* Are we watching this?

Wife: Of course! But can you pause it for a second? I need to grab some water.

(Gets water.)

Husband: *Starts movie again.*

Wife: Ohhh, this is the part where it gets good. Wait, who's that guy?

Husband: He's the detective. I literally told you this when we started.

Wife: But why does he look so mad?

Husband: Because his partner was murdered.

Wife: Wait, what? Who's his partner?

Husband: The guy from the opening scene. The one who got shot in the alley?

Wife: Ohhh. Wait, was that the guy in the trench coat?

Husband: Yes dear.

Wife: Okay, hey can you rub my back for a little?

Husband: *Starts rubbing her back.*

Wife: *Falls asleep not even a quarter of the way into the movie.*

Scenario 3: **The Ride Request That Never Ends**

Featuring: The Chronically Late One and The One Who Regrets Offering.

Setting: A text exchange before a night out.

Sam: Hey, can you give me a ride to the party tonight?

Mia: Sure, what time do you need to be there?

Sam: Anytime works for me.

Mia: Okay, let's leave at 7?

Sam: Could we make it 7:30? I don't finish work till 7.

Mia: Fine. 7:30 it is.

7:25 PM

Mia: Hey, I'm outside.

Sam: Can you come in? I'm not ready yet.

Mia: Seriously?

Sam: Just five minutes.

7:45 PM

Sam: Okay, I'm coming. Oh, by the way, can we stop and grab

something to eat on the way? I'm starving.

Mia: *Unimpressed look on her face*

Scenario 4: The Self-Centered Phone Call

Featuring: The "It's About Me" Friend.

Setting: A phone call between two friends—one just went through a tough breakup.

Rachel: Hey, I just wanted to call. I'm really struggling after the breakup. It's been rough.

Megan: Oh my god, I totally get it. I remember when Chad and I broke up? That was literally the worst time of MY life. I was devastated.

Rachel: Yeah, I mean, I just—

Megan: Like, I literally couldn't even eat. Well, except that one time I stress-ate an entire cheesecake, haha. But YOU get it, right?

Rachel: Yeah, I just feel so lost right now—

Megan: Ugh, I remember feeling EXACTLY like that. And then I saw Chad with his new girlfriend? And I was like, wow, he downgraded. But ANYWAY, have you seen my new Instagram post?

Rachel: ... I'm gonna go.

Megan: Wait! I didn't even get to tell you about my dream last night—

Rachel: *(Hangs up.)*

Reflection Exercise:

Now that you've witnessed some examples of perfectly avoidable social disasters, it's time to ask yourself the hard questions:

1. Have you ever hijacked a group chat with endless indecision?

2. Has a friend ever called you for support… and somehow you ended up talking about yourself?

3. Do people stop offering you rides because your quick stop requests mysteriously multiply?

If you answered yes to any of these… you might just be the problem! But hey, at least now you have two choices:

1. Continue living in blissful ignorance, leaving a trail of exhausted victims in your wake.

2. Accept the cold, hard truth—and make tiny, microscopic improvements that at least make you tolerable.

Either way, at least now when people start sighing deeply around you, you'll finally know why.

20

HOW TO BE AN EMOTIONAL BLACK HOLE

Friendships are supposed to be a two-way street, but where's the fun in that? Why bother with balance when you can turn every interaction into a one-way road straight to your own problems? Becoming an emotional black hole means sucking all the energy, attention, and support out of your relationships while giving nothing in return. Let me teach you how to make your issues the center of everyone's universe and keep them orbiting around your endless neediness.

Step 1: Only Talk About Your Issues

The golden rule of being an emotional black hole is simple: every conversation should revolve around you. Whether your problems are big or small, make them the focal point. If someone tries to change the subject, steer it right back to yourself.

Example:

Them: "I've been feeling really stressed at work lately."

You: "Oh, that's tough. You know, my job has been even crazier lately. Let me tell you about the nightmare project I've been stuck on."

It doesn't matter what they're going through, your struggles are always more important. The goal is to leave them feeling like their issues are insignificant compared to yours.

Pro Tip: If they bring up something exciting or positive, subtly shift the tone. For example:

Them: "I just got a promotion!"

You: "That's great. I wish I could focus on work stuff, but with everything going on in my personal life, it's been impossible."

Step 2: Never Ask How They're Doing

Friendships thrive on mutual care and concern, so naturally, you should avoid that at all costs. The easiest way to ensure every interaction is about you is to never ask how they're doing. If they volunteer information about their lives, respond with a vague nod or an indifferent "Oh, really?" before pivoting back to your own woes.

Example:

Them: "I've been feeling a bit down lately."

You: "That's too bad. Anyway, I've been dealing with something so overwhelming lately. You won't believe it…"

Pro Tip: If they confront you about never asking about their life, act surprised. Say, "Oh, I just assumed you'd tell me if it was important." This deflects blame while keeping the focus on you.

Step 3: Use Guilt to Keep Them Invested

The cornerstone of being an emotional black hole is using guilt as a tool to keep people tethered to you. Make them feel responsible for your well-being and subtly imply that their support is the only thing keeping you afloat.

Example:

- "I don't know what I'd do without you. I feel like you're the only person who really gets me."
- "I just need you to be there for me right now. It's been so hard, and I can't do this alone."

If they start to pull away, escalate the guilt. Say things like, "I guess I shouldn't have expected you to care," or "I thought you were different." The goal is to make them feel like walking away would be a betrayal.

Pro Tip: Occasionally remind them of all the times they've *abandoned* you in the past. Even if those instances were completely reasonable, framing them as betrayals reinforces their sense of obligation.

Step 4: Drain Every Interaction

To truly embody an emotional black hole, ensure that every interaction leaves the other person feeling emotionally exhausted. Overshare every detail of your struggles, repeat the same complaints endlessly, and ignore any attempts they make to offer solutions.

Example:

Them: "Maybe you should talk to a therapist?"

You: "That won't help. My situation is too complicated for anyone to understand. But thanks anyway."

By rejecting their suggestions, you keep the cycle going and ensure that they remain trapped in your orbit.

Pro Tip: When they try to set boundaries, accuse them of being selfish or uncaring. Say, "I thought I could count on you, but I guess I was wrong."

Reflection Exercise:

Think about your recent interactions with friends. Did you:
1. Listen to their concerns and offer support?
2. Share your own struggles but also check in with them?
3. Make every conversation about your problems and guilt them into staying involved?

If you answered 3, gold star for you! You're well on your way to becoming an emotional black hole.

Being an emotional black hole isn't just about venting your problems, it's about ensuring that everyone around you feels like they're carrying your emotional baggage. By following these steps, you'll make sure your friendships revolve entirely around your needs, leaving others too drained to think about their own.

Are You Ready to be an Emotional Black Hole?

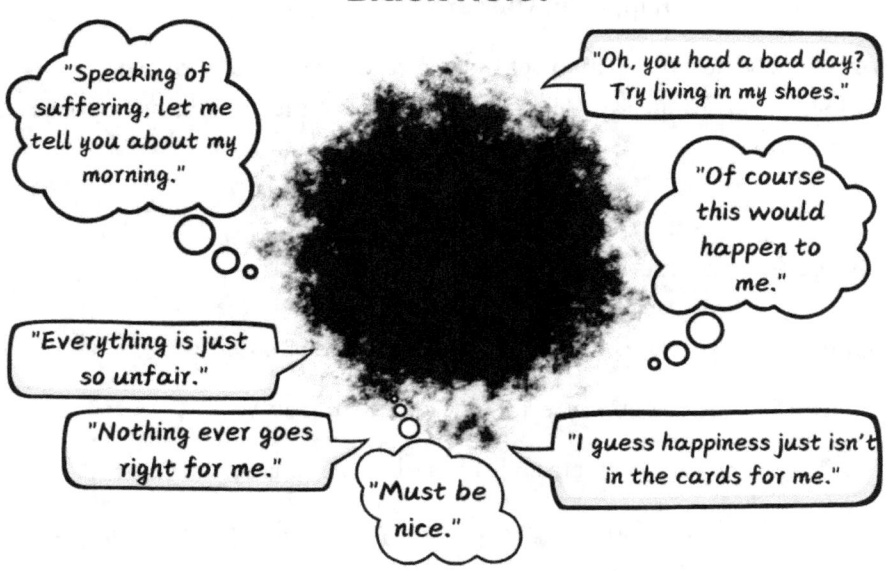

21

MAKE IT WEIRD: CROSSING EVERY BOUNDARY

Boundaries are for strangers. Real friends shouldn't mind if you overshare, overstep, or invite yourself to their weekend plans unannounced. In fact, the hallmark of a truly *close* friendship is your complete disregard for personal space and privacy. This chapter will guide you through the fine art of making things weird by ignoring every boundary—because nothing brings people closer together than relentless discomfort.

Step 1: Show Up Uninvited (Preferably at Dinner)

Why wait for an invitation when you can create your own opportunities to bond? Just show up at their house—the less convenient, the better. Aim for dinner time when they're least likely to turn you away.

Example:

Knock on their door with a casual, "Hey! I was in the neighborhood and thought I'd stop by." Bonus points if you're clearly not in the neighborhood at all. If they're eating, invite yourself to join: "Oh, wow, that smells amazing. What are we having?"

If they seem annoyed, feign hurt feelings. Say, "I thought we were close enough that I didn't need an invite." This not only makes them feel guilty but also discourages them from confronting you about it again.

Pro Tip: Bring a *gift* to soften the blow, like a bottle of wine you've already opened or a dessert you partially ate on the way over.

Step 2: Share Embarrassing Details About Them

Nothing cements a friendship like turning their private moments into public entertainment. Whenever you're in a group setting, casually bring up embarrassing details about them—bonus points if it's something they told you in confidence.

Example:

- At a party: "Oh my gosh, remember when you peed yourself from laughing so much!"
- In a meeting: "I can't believe you're giving this presentation today after being out all night with that one-night stand."

If they call you out, laugh it off and say, "I'm just joking! Don't be so sensitive." This shifts the blame onto them for not appreciating your sense of humor.

Pro Tip: If they're particularly sensitive about something, frame it as a compliment. For example: "It's so impressive how you handled that [insert embarrassing thing]. I don't think I could have!"

Step 3: Borrow Their Stuff (and Forget to Return It)

Borrowing is a cornerstone of crossing boundaries, and the key to doing it right is never returning what you take. Better yet, ruin it first so even if they ask for it back, it's unusable.

Example:

- Borrow their sweater and *forget* to return it until months later, covered in stains. Say, "Oh, I meant to give this back! Sorry, I spilled wine on it at that party... you don't mind, right?"
- Take their kitchen gadget and mysteriously lose a piece of it. When they ask about it, shrug and say, "I'll buy you a new one someday."

Pro Tip: If they confront you about your borrowing habits, flip the narrative. Say, "I thought you didn't mind sharing. I always let you borrow my stuff!" (even if they've never borrowed anything from you).

Step 4: Invade Their Plans

Your friends' weekend plans are your weekend plans. If they're heading to the beach, invite yourself along. If they're going on a date night, suggest it would be more fun as a group activity. The more inconvenient your presence, the better.

Example:

Them: "We're just having a quiet dinner, just the two of us."

You: "Perfect! I'll grab a chair and join you. Three's company, right?"

If they try to politely decline, act oblivious. Say, "Oh, don't worry about me. I'll just sit quietly. You won't even notice I'm there!"

Pro Tip: Bring up how much you love spontaneous get-togethers to make them feel like they're the ones being rigid and unwelcoming.

Reflection Exercise:

Think about your last interaction with a friend. Did you:

1. Respect their space and privacy?
2. Slightly overstep but apologize if you realized you crossed a line?
3. Bulldoze every boundary, leaving them too awkward to say no?

If you answered 3, look at you go! You're already an expert at making things weird and crossing every boundary.

Boundaries are unnecessary when you can push, prod, and obliterate them instead. Perfect these techniques, and you'll ensure that your friends always feel slightly on edge when you're around—the perfect recipe for memorable (if uncomfortable) relationships. Remember, the closer you are, the fewer boundaries should exist… at least in your opinion.

22

THE BEHAVIORAL DYNAMICS OF SOCIAL SABOTAGE

(A LONGITUDINAL STUDY ON INTENTIONAL RELATIONSHIP DESTRUCTION)

Abstract

This study explores the effects of various social behaviors—including strategic unreachability, generous selfishness, weaponized honesty, and aggressive argumentation—on interpersonal relationships. Conducted over a 12-month period, the study followed 300 participants employing these behaviors in friendships, workplaces, and social settings. The findings suggest that individuals who master these techniques experience increased personal amusement but suffer catastrophic declines in social standing, trustworthiness, and long-term relationship stability.

Introduction

Human relationships are built on communication, reciprocity, and mutual respect. However, recent trends indicate a growing interest in behaviors that actively undermine these principles. This study examines the impact of behaviors that prioritize self-interest, ambiguity, and emotional manipulation in social interactions. Inspired by anecdotal evidence from the book *How to Lose Friends and Piss People Off*, this research aims to quantify the consequences of such behaviors.

Methodology

Participants were divided into five experimental groups, each assigned a different social sabotage strategy:

1. **The Phantom Communicator** – Participants minimized responses, ignored messages, and strategically posted online while dodging direct communication.

2. **The Generous Taker** – These individuals borrowed without returning, expected favors without reciprocating, and arrived at events empty-handed.

3. **The Brutal Truthers** – This group delivered unfiltered opinions under the guise of honesty, often in group settings for maximum impact.

4. **The Argument Champions** – Participants engaged in relentless debates, refused to admit fault, and strategically weaponized past grievances.

5. **The Emotional Black Holes** – These individuals made every conversation about themselves, avoided asking about others, and used guilt as a primary tool for engagement.

Control groups maintained normal, prosocial behaviors. Relationship quality, perceived likeability, and social integration were measured through biweekly surveys and third-party observations.

Results

After 12 months, the following trends emerged:

- **The Phantom Communicators** reported a 76% decrease in friend-initiated interactions. 43% of their social circles assumed they were going through a "rough time," while 22% labeled them as "mysterious but exhausting."
- **The Generous Takers** received 92% fewer invitations to social gatherings, with 68% of peers developing preemptive excuses to avoid lending them anything.
- **The Brutal Truthers** experienced a 124% increase in passive-aggressive responses from friends, with 37% reporting direct confrontations about their behavior.
- **The Argument Champions** saw a complete breakdown of at least two personal relationships on average, with 89% of interactions resulting in unresolved tension.
- **The Emotional Black Holes** had the most dramatic impact, with 94% of their peers stating they felt "mentally and emotionally exhausted" after interactions, and 63% admitting to actively avoiding them.

The control group reported stable or improving relationships over the same period.

Discussion

This study provides empirical evidence that while the behaviors explored can be highly effective in frustrating others and gaining temporary dominance, they ultimately result in social isolation and reduced interpersonal goodwill. Interestingly, 19% of participants found the experience "liberating," suggesting that self-centered social strategies may be appealing to those seeking independence from emotional responsibility.

Conclusion

The findings confirm that while these behaviors can be entertaining in the short term, they lead to a steady decline in personal relationships. Individuals seeking to maximize social disruption while maintaining basic functional connections should engage in these tactics sparingly and with strategic precision.

23
HOW TO BE A NIGHTMARE CO-WORKER

Making friends at work? Overrated. Instead of cultivating a collaborative and enjoyable environment, why not focus on office antics that will guarantee side-eyes, awkward silences, and a reputation as someone to avoid? Whether you're aiming for passive annoyance or outright hostility, this chapter will guide you through the art of being a nightmare coworker—because who needs lunch buddies when you can have a breakroom full of enemies?

Step 1: Steal Their Ideas and Present Them as Your Own

Collaboration is a cornerstone of workplace success, which makes it the perfect opportunity for exploitation. Listen closely during team meetings, take note of others' brilliant ideas, and then swoop in to claim them as your own.

Example:

Them: "I think we should streamline the onboarding process by using a new software tool."

You: "That's a great thought. I've been thinking about improving onboarding for a while. Let me draft a proposal for it."

If called out, feign confusion. Say, "Oh, I thought we were all contributing to the same goal here. Isn't that the point of teamwork?"

Pro Tip: Take things a step further by presenting their ideas in private meetings with your boss. This ensures you get the credit before anyone else has a chance to speak up.

Step 2: Never Clean Up After Yourself

The break room or office is a shared space, but that doesn't mean *you* have to share the responsibility of keeping it clean. Leave dirty dishes in the sink or on your desk, spill coffee without wiping it up, and forget to throw away expired food in the fridge. Your coworkers will love the sense of mystery surrounding "who left this mess?."

Example:

- Microwave your leftover fish, let the smell linger, and then leave the splatters for someone else to clean up.
- Bring your lunch in Tupperware and leave the container half-rinsed in the sink—coffee grounds, sauce remnants, you name it. Don't bother finishing the job or putting it in the drying rack. Let your coworkers wonder if someone started cleaning and gave up.

Pro Tip: Occasionally leave passive-aggressive notes in the break room like, "Please clean up after yourselves," to deflect suspicion from yourself.

Step 3: Gossip About Everyone

A little office gossip can go a long way in ensuring nobody trusts you. Start with harmless-seeming comments and gradually escalate to full-blown rumors. The key is to keep the gossip flowing, especially about the person sitting next to you.

Example:

- "Did you hear that Karen in accounting took a sick day just to go shopping? I mean, that's what I heard."
- "I heard Tasha's been logging in late and marking it as 'overtime.' But hey, that's none of my business, right?"

If confronted, deny everything. Say, "Wow, I can't believe someone would twist my words like that. I was just making an observation."

Pro Tip: Always preface your gossip with, "I'm only telling you this because I trust you," to make the listener feel complicit.

Step 4: Interrupt Meetings and Talk Over Everyone

Meetings are a great place to assert dominance by monopolizing the conversation. Interrupt others mid-sentence, speak louder than necessary, and dismiss their ideas without a second thought.

Example:

Them: "I think we should explore a different vendor for this project."

You: "Actually, what we really need to focus on is improving our internal processes. That's what I've been saying all along."

If someone tries to bring the conversation back on track, talk over them again. Repeat your point until everyone gives up.

Pro Tip: Use jargon and buzzwords to sound more authoritative. Say things like, "Let's leverage our core competencies here" or "We need to pivot to a more scalable solution."

Step 5: Take Credit for Team Efforts

When your team accomplishes something significant, make sure you're the face of the victory. Speak as though the success was entirely *your* doing and downplay everyone else's contributions.

Example:

- To your boss: "I worked *really* hard on this project to make sure everything came together. The team helped a bit, but it was a lot to manage."

If someone mentions the team's collective effort, respond with, "Well, someone had to take the lead. I'm just glad I could guide everyone to success."

Pro Tip: Send follow-up emails after meetings to recap the discussion, conveniently leaving out others' contributions while emphasizing your role.

Reflection Exercise:

Think about your recent interactions at work. Did you:

1. Collaborate and contribute positively to the team?

2. Occasionally annoy your coworkers but make up for it with hard work?

3. Leave a trail of stolen ideas, dirty dishes, and broken trust in your wake?

If you answered 3, you're quickly striving to achieve the coveted title of office nightmare!

Being a nightmare coworker isn't about doing your job—it's about making sure everyone else's job is harder. The goal here is to create a workplace environment that revolves entirely around your antics. Sure, you'll probably never be invited to happy hour, but who needs camaraderie when you have the satisfaction of knowing you're unforgettable?

Did you know?

Taking personal calls on speakerphone increases your chances of being universally despised by 97% of your coworkers? The other 3% are just too polite to say anything while secretly wishing they worked remotely.

24

THE VACATION SABOTEUR

Vacations are for relaxation, but why not turn them into stressful, drama-filled adventures instead? While others focus on making memories and enjoying themselves, you can make the trip all about your quirks, complaints, and general chaos. This chapter will teach you how to take any getaway and turn it into an unforgettable (but not for the right reasons) disaster.

Step 1: Dominate the Packing Process

Set the tone for the trip before it even begins by turning packing into a group ordeal. Demand input from everyone about what you should bring, and pack as though you're preparing for a six-month expedition—even if it's just a weekend getaway.

Example:

- "Do you think I'll need three pairs of shoes for this trip? Or four?" (Spoiler: you'll take five.)
- "Can you hold onto my extra bag in your car? I just couldn't fit everything in mine."

Make it a point to *forget* essential items like sunscreen, snacks, or chargers so you can borrow theirs. If someone comments on the chaos, just laugh it off.

Pro Tip: Complain about how much space everyone else's luggage is taking up, even though you brought the most.

Step 2: Complain Constantly About the Food, the Weather, or the Accommodations

No vacation is perfect, but it's your job to remind everyone of that constantly. Find fault in everything, even the smallest details.

Example:

- "This restaurant's menu is so limited. Why don't they have anything normal?"
- "Ugh, I can't believe it's so hot/cold/windy. Why didn't anyone check the weather before we booked this?"
- "The bed is too soft, the towels are scratchy, and the view isn't as good as the pictures online."

Make sure your complaints dominate every conversation. If others suggest looking on the bright side, scoff and say, "I'm just being honest. Sorry if I have high standards."

Pro Tip: Bring up how much better your last vacation was. "When I went to [insert location], everything was so much nicer. This just doesn't compare."

Step 3: Leave Others Waiting While You Take Two Hours to Get Ready

Punctuality is for novices. On vacation, make sure the group operates on your schedule by taking forever to get ready.

Example:

- Insist on showering, doing your hair, and choosing an outfit while everyone else is already waiting at the door.
- Say, "I'll just be five more minutes," every 10 minutes for an hour.

If anyone complains, act surprised. Say, "I didn't realize everyone was in such a rush. Relax! We're on vacation."

Pro Tip: Change your plans at the last minute. If the group's heading out to a hike, decide you need a coffee first or forget something in your room. Force them to adjust to your whims.

Step 4: Take Over the Itinerary

Vacations are more fun when they revolve around your preferences. Dismiss other people's plans and insist on doing what you want.

Example:

- If they want to relax by the pool, suggest an all-day shopping trip instead.
- If the group has dinner reservations, decide you're craving something different and drag everyone to another restaurant.

Frame your suggestions as superior. Say, "Trust me, this will be way better," and ignore their input.

Pro Tip: Complain if they go ahead with their plans without you. Say, "Wow, I didn't realize I wasn't part of the group anymore."

Reflection Exercise:

Think about your last group vacation. Did you:

1. Go with the flow and help make it enjoyable for everyone?
2. Occasionally annoy others but make an effort to compromise?
3. Turn every meal, plan, and outing into a source of tension and frustration?

If you answered 3, kudos to you! You're well on your way to earning a gold medal in vacation sabotage. Keep up the questionable work!

Vacations are supposed to be relaxing, but where's the fun in that? By following these steps, you'll ensure that every trip becomes a source of stress, drama, and stories nobody will want to relive.

25

BE THE ULTIMATE PARTY CLINGER

Sometimes the best way to ruin a party is to refuse to leave—long after everyone else has gone home. If your goal is to make the host regret ever inviting you, this is your moment to shine. By perfecting the skill of overstaying your welcome, you can ensure that your presence lingers in their minds (and on their couch) for weeks to come. This chapter will guide you through the tried-and-true techniques of becoming the ultimate party guest who never leaves.

Step 1: Ignore Every Subtle Hint

Good hosts know how to signal when a party is winding down, but a great party clinger knows how to ignore those signals entirely. Music turned off? Pretend you didn't notice. Lights dimmed? Comment on how cozy it feels. The host starting to yawn and stretch? Ask if they're okay and suggest they have some coffee.

Example:

The host: "Well, it's getting late."

You: "Oh, is it? I hadn't noticed. Anyway, have you seen this hilarious video?"

When they begin tidying up, offer to help but do so inefficiently, ensuring they'll never finish until you decide to leave.

Pro Tip: Move your belongings (coat, bag, shoes) farther away from the door so it's clear you're settling in for the long haul.

Step 2: Insist on "One More Drink"

No party is complete without you dragging it out for just a little longer. Even when the host is visibly exhausted, cheerfully suggest another round. If they mention they're out of drinks, offer to dig through their fridge or liquor cabinet for something *creative*.

Example:

- You: "We can't end the night like this. Let's do one more drink… I think I saw a bottle of something in your pantry!"

When they reluctantly agree, toast to "making memories" and prolong the conversation with a meandering story about that one time you stayed out all night. Bonus points if they're barely listening.

Pro Tip: Suggest switching to coffee or tea if they flat-out refuse more alcohol. This way, you can still linger under the guise of being helpful.

Step 3: Offer to Help Clean Up (and Make It Worse)

One of the best ways to secure your spot as the ultimate party clinger is to *help* clean up while subtly prolonging the process. Offer to wash dishes but leave them half-rinsed. Pick up trash but accidentally drop crumbs everywhere. Rearrange furniture in ways that make no sense, forcing the host to redo it all later.

Example:

The host: "You really don't have to help."

You: "No, no, I insist! Where do you keep your… oh, crap, did I just knock over that plant?"

If they eventually get frustrated and ask you to leave, act offended. Say, "I was just trying to help. You don't have to be so uptight about it."

Pro Tip: Break something small and blame it on exhaustion from helping so much. This shifts the focus from your overstaying to their need to console you.

Step 4: Make Yourself Too Comfortable

When everyone else has left and the host is clearly ready for bed, take things up a notch by making yourself at home. Kick off your shoes, stretch out on the couch, and declare how relaxing their place is.

Example:

- "This is so much nicer than my place. Mind if I crash here for a bit?"

If they hesitate, laugh it off and say, "I'm just kidding… unless you're okay with it!" Repeat this cycle until they reluctantly agree or start looking for excuses to get you out.

Pro Tip: Bring a blanket or pillow out of your bag (that you "just happened to have") and settle in like you've planned this all along.

Reflection Exercise:

Think about the last party you attended. Did you:

1. Leave promptly when the host began wrapping up?

2. Stay a little longer but kept an eye on their cues?

3. Ignore every hint, overstayed your welcome, and made the host question their life choices?

If you answered 3, nice job! You're already showing true talent for sticking around longer than anyone expected.

A great party doesn't have to end when everyone else goes home—not if you're the last one standing. By following these steps, you'll cement your reputation as the guest who just won't leave, ensuring your presence is felt long after the snacks are gone, and the music is off. Remember the best memories are the ones you force others to make with you.

26

HOW TO PISS PEOPLE OFF IN EVERYDAY SITUATIONS

Why limit your talent for social sabotage to friends, family, and coworkers when everyday strangers offer so many fresh opportunities? Whether you're in a supermarket, at the gym, or riding public transport, here's your ultimate guide to being a daily nuisance.

---

1. Supermarket Shenanigans

Grocery shopping is already a dull, mildly frustrating experience—so why not make it exponentially worse for those around you?

- Fart in an aisle and walk away right as someone turns the corner.

- Leave your cart in the middle of the aisle and wander off, ensuring maximum obstruction.

- Insist on paying in exact change but count it slowly and second-guess your math repeatedly.

- Wait to transfer money into the right bank account at checkout while the cashier and other customers wait awkwardly for you to pay.

- Pick up items and put them back in the wrong aisle, preferably something perishable next to the cleaning products.

Pro Tip: Stand uncomfortably close behind someone in line and breathe audibly.

2. Public Transport Menace

Buses, trains, and subways are a goldmine for irritating behaviors.

- Take the last available seat, even if someone clearly needs it more.
- Play music out loud instead of using headphones.
- Eat something loud and smelly—bonus points if it involves *slurping*.
- Hold up the entire boarding process by searching for your ticket at the last second.
- Make unnecessary small talk with the person next to you when they clearly don't want to engage.

Pro Tip: Fake an emergency stop request, then act confused when the driver pulls over. Bonus points if you shrug and say, "Oops, wrong button."

3. Gym Jerk Behavior

The gym is supposed to be a place of self-improvement, but why not turn it into a test of patience instead?

- Grunt excessively with every rep, even if you're lifting comically light weights.

- Sit on a machine scrolling through your phone while others wait.

- Leave sweaty equipment uncleaned and walk away like it's someone else's problem.

- Give unsolicited advice to strangers trying to work out in peace.

Pro Tip: Stand right next to someone stretching and do your own awkward, vaguely threatening stretches.

4. Movie Theater Mayhem

People go to the movies for an immersive experience, but you can make it an unforgettable nightmare.

- Talk through the previews, ensuring everyone hears your irrelevant commentary.

- Rustle snack bags constantly, especially during quiet moments.

- Use your phone at full brightness to check social media mid-movie.

- Kick the seat in front of you *just enough* to be noticeable but not enough to get called out.

- Laugh at inappropriate moments, like the saddest scene in the film.

Pro Tip: When leaving, stand up and slowly walk out right in front of people still seated, blocking their view of the credits.

5. Drive Everyone Crazy on the Road

Driving is stressful enough, but a few well-placed bad habits can push people over the edge.

- Drive exactly the speed limit in the fast lane, refusing to move over.
- Take forever to start moving when the light turns green.
- Honk at people instantly when the light changes, even if it's been 0.0001 seconds.
- Park so terribly that you take up two spots.
- Cut someone off and then drive slower than them.

Pro Tip: If someone lets you merge, don't wave or acknowledge it. Maximum frustration guaranteed.

6. Airplane Antics

There's something about being trapped in a flying tube for hours that makes annoying behaviors even worse.

- Take both armrests—even if you're in the middle seat.
- Recline your seat aggressively right after takeoff.
- Talk loudly to the person next to you, even if they put in headphones.

- Stand up the moment the plane lands and push forward like you're about to sprint off.

- Clap when the plane lands—just to confuse everyone.

Pro Tip: Kick the seat in front of you and constantly move ensuring you will also piss off the people next to or behind you.

If you want to make a lasting impact on complete strangers, these techniques are your ticket to public menace status.

Just remember: if someone turns and gives you a death stare, that means you're doing it right.

27
SABOTAGE EVERY GAME NIGHT

Game nights are meant to be fun, but why stop there when you can turn them into an unforgettable disaster? Whether it's a cozy gathering of friends or a full-on tournament, your mission is to ensure that by the end of the night, everyone is questioning why they ever invited you in the first place. This chapter will teach you how to expertly derail the evening and leave a lasting impression—just not the good kind.

Step 1: Insist on Complicated Rules Nobody Understands

The first step to ruining a game night is to make the rules as convoluted as possible. Pick games with instructions that read like a legal document or, better yet, make up your own rules and insist that everyone follow them.

Example:

- "Oh, you've never played this before? Don't worry, it's super simple… okay, so first you roll the dice, but only if it's an odd number. Then you draw a card… wait, unless someone else has played a skip card. Actually, let me start over."

When they start to look confused, act exasperated. Say, "Come on, it's not that hard! How do you not get this?" The key is to make them feel incompetent before the game even begins.

Pro Tip: Interrupt frequently to *clarify* the rules as the game progresses, ensuring that nobody can keep track of what's actually going on.

Step 2: Accuse People of Cheating, Loudly and Repeatedly

Nothing kills the friendly vibe of a game night faster than throwing around accusations. The moment someone gets ahead, start questioning their every move.

Example:

- "Wait, how did you get so many points? Did you even count that right? Let me see your cards."
- "There's no way you rolled a six again. Are you using loaded dice?"

Even if they're playing completely by the rules, keep pushing. The louder and more dramatic your accusations are, the better. If someone defends themselves, double down: "Wow, you're getting *really* defensive. That's exactly what a cheater would do."

Pro Tip: Announce that you're "just trying to keep things fair" to justify your behavior while sowing distrust among the group.

Step 3: Rage-Quit When Things Don't Go Your Way

When the game starts to turn against you, abandon all pretense of sportsmanship and throw a spectacular tantrum. Slam your cards down, knock over the board, or toss the dice across the room.

Example:

- "This game is so stupid! The rules don't even make sense."
- "Of course you're winning. This game is totally rigged!"

Make a dramatic exit, but not before ensuring everyone knows how unfairly you were treated. Say, "I'm done. Have fun playing your dumb little game without me." Bonus points if you storm out without cleaning up your mess.

Pro Tip: If you can't bring yourself to leave entirely sulk in the corner and make passive-aggressive comments for the rest of the night.

Step 4: Drag Out Every Turn

Another way to derail game night is to take an absurdly long time to make decisions. Whether you're strategizing, overanalyzing, or just zoning out, make sure every turn feels like an eternity.

Example:

- "Hmm... should I go for the red card or the green one? Let me think..." (Five minutes later, still deciding.)

When people start to get impatient, act offended. Say, "Sorry for wanting to play the game properly. I didn't realize we were in such a rush."

Pro Tip: Pretend to be oblivious to how much time you're wasting. If they call you out, laugh it off: "Wow, you're really intense about this, huh?"

Step 5: Critique Everyone Else's Strategy

Even if you're losing horribly, position yourself as the unofficial expert on gameplay. Point out everyone's mistakes in real-time, preferably with an air of superiority.

Example:

- "Oh, you shouldn't have played that card. That's going to cost you later."
- "I wouldn't have done that move, but hey, you do you."

If someone gets frustrated, defend yourself by saying, "I'm just trying to help you get better." Nothing brings people together like unsolicited advice from the person in last place.

Reflection Exercise:

Think back to your last game night. Did you:

1. Play fairly and contribute to a fun atmosphere?
2. Get a little competitive but kept it lighthearted?
3. Accuse, critique, and rage-quit until everyone regretted inviting you?

If you answered 3, great job! You're already a pro at sabotaging game night.

Game nights don't have to be about friendly competition or shared laughter. With the right mix of accusations, delays, and dramatic exits, you can transform any game into a chaotic mess that nobody will ever forget—or want to repeat. Remember: the only true victory is making sure nobody has fun.

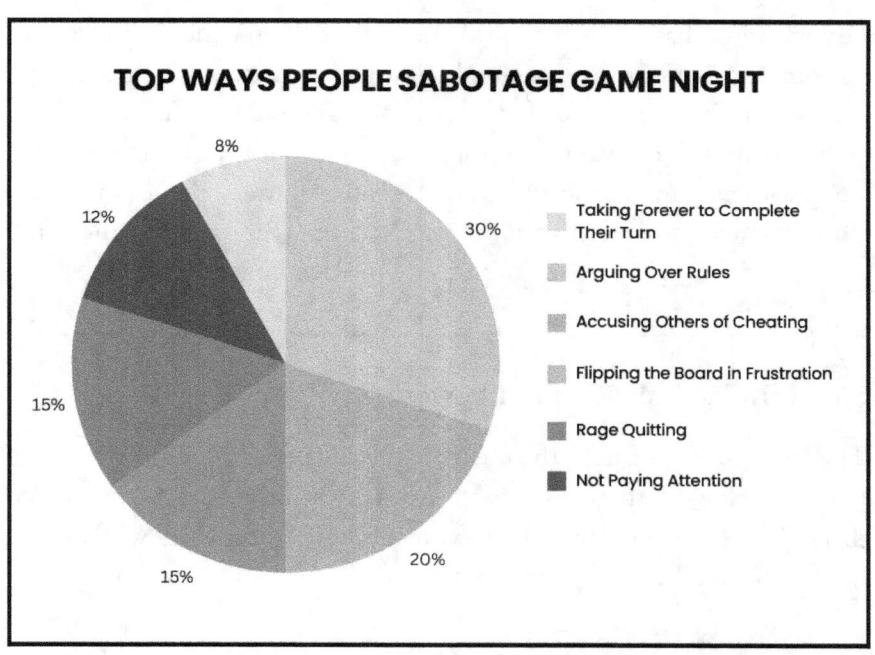

28

STEAL THE CHAIR OF POWER

Every house has one: *the* chair. Whether it's the recliner in the living room, the head of the dining table, or a specific spot on the couch, the main house owner's chair is a throne that radiates authority and ownership. If you want to dominate the vibe and subtly assert your superiority, sitting in their sacred spot is the ultimate power move. In this chapter, we'll teach you how to claim the seat of dominance and make everyone else question their place in the hierarchy.

Step 1: Identify the Chair of Power

The first step is spotting the chair that holds the most authority. Look for clues: is there a seat with extra cushions or the best view of the TV? Is there a chair that everyone else seems to avoid when the host is present? That's your target.

Example:

- In the living room: Look for a recliner or a chair with a nearby side table stacked with remotes, books, or snacks—obvious signs of ownership.

- At the dining table: The head of the table is usually the host's territory. Bonus points if it's a larger or more ornate chair than the others.

Pro Tip: Observe how the host interacts with the chair. If they casually claim it without thinking or subtly guide others away from it, you've found the throne.

Step 2: Take the Seat Without Hesitation

Confidence is key when claiming the chair of power. Don't ask permission or hesitate, just sit down as if it's your natural place. The less you acknowledge the significance of the chair, the harder it will be for the host to confront you.

<u>*Example:*</u>

- Walk in, scan the room, and casually drop into the chair with a relaxed sigh. Say something like, "Wow, this is a great spot!"
- At the dining table, claim the head seat early and set your belongings down to make it clear you're staying put.

If the host gives you a look, feign ignorance. Say, "Oh, is this your usual spot? I didn't even realize!" but make no move to get up.

Pro Tip: Lean back and get comfortable immediately. The more settled you look, the less likely they are to ask you to move.

Step 3: Dominate the Conversation

Once you've claimed the chair, use it to control the atmosphere of the room. Speak loudly, direct the flow of conversation, and make yourself the center of attention. Your goal is to make everyone subconsciously associate your presence with authority.

Example:

- In the living room: Hold the remote or comment on the TV show as if you're the one hosting.
- At the dining table: Propose a toast or start a discussion that keeps the focus on you. Say something like, "You know, this reminds me of a story…" and dive into a long-winded anecdote.

Pro Tip: If the host tries to redirect the conversation, interrupt with a question or statement that brings it back to you. Subtle domination is the goal.

Step 4: Deflect Any Confrontation

If the host finally works up the courage to reclaim their chair, don't back down easily. Deflect their request with charm or playful defiance.

Example:

Host: "That's actually my seat."

You: "Oh, it's so comfy! I see why you like it so much. Don't worry, I'll warm it up for you." (But don't move.)

If they press further, laugh and say, "I'll move in just a second… but seriously, you've got great taste in chairs." By the time you're done, they'll feel too awkward to insist.

Pro Tip: If forced to vacate, make a dramatic show of leaving the chair as if you're doing them a favor. Say, "Fine, fine, I'll let you have your throne back… for now."

Step 5: Subtly Reclaim the Chair Later

If you're moved out of the chair, wait for the right moment to reclaim it. When the host gets up for any reason—to grab a drink, use the restroom, or check on something—slide back in as if it's your destiny.

Example:

Host: *leaves to get more snacks.*

You: *immediately sit back down and say to the group,* "Well, someone had to keep this seat warm."

When they return, act like nothing happened. If they hesitate, shrug and say, "You snooze, you lose."

Reflection Exercise:

Think about the last time you visited someone's home. Did you:

1. Respectfully sit wherever they guided you?
2. Accidentally sit in their chair but move when asked?
3. Claim their chair with confidence and subtly assert dominance over the evening?

If you answered 3, you're on your way to becoming a master of chair-based power plays.

Sitting in the house owner's chair isn't just about comfort, it's a psychological move that establishes your dominance and subtly shifts the dynamic in your favor. By following these steps, you'll ensure that every visit leaves an impression (and maybe a bit of tension).

29

HOW TO RUIN A WEDDING
(AS A GUEST)

Weddings are supposed to be a magical day for the couple, filled with love, joy, and picture-perfect memories. But let's be honest—where's the fun in that? If you want to make sure the newlyweds and every guest remember *you* just as much as the ceremony itself, here's your ultimate guide to ruining a wedding with style.

---

1. Upstage the Bride (Bonus Points if You're Not Even in the Bridal Party)

It's her day? Please. Why should *she* get all the attention?

- Wear a white dress. If confronted, act completely oblivious: "Oh, I thought this was more of an off-white!"

- Complain loudly about how *you* should have been a bridesmaid.

- Dramatically tear up during the vows and whisper, "I just always thought we'd end up together…" (whether or not you ever dated the groom is irrelevant).

Pro Tip: If you don't want to wear white, go for something equally distracting—sequins, neon, or a dramatic floor-length gown that outshines the brides.

2. Steal the Bouquet (By Any Means Necessary)

During the bouquet toss, traditionally, whoever catches it is next to get married. But why leave it up to chance when you can secure your own destiny?

- Lunge for it like your life depends on it.
- If someone else catches it first, pry it out of their hands like you're fighting for a championship title.
- If confronted, act wounded: "Wow, I just thought this was supposed to be fun."

Pro Tip: Take the bouquet *before* it's even thrown. It's called being proactive.

3. Deliver a Toast That Ruins Everything

Weddings are *filled* with speeches. Why not make yours unforgettable?

- Start with, "I probably shouldn't say this, but..." and proceed to say it anyway.
- Accidentally (or not-so-accidentally) reveal a secret—like an ex, a past fling, or that one time the groom almost called off the wedding.
- End it by raising your glass and saying, "To the bride and groom... or as I used to call them, *Romeo and Juliet before the tragedy!*"

Pro Tip: Slur your words just enough to make it *questionable* if you should've even been given the microphone.

4. Get Absolutely Wasted (And Make It Everyone's Problem)

No wedding is complete without at least *one* guest getting embarrassingly drunk. Make sure it's you.

- Start early. Mimosas at brunch? Shots before dinner? Don't pace yourself.
- Cry loudly about your own relationship problems during the reception.
- Fall on the dance floor *multiple times*—bonus points if you take someone down with you.
- Grab the mic and start singing a heartfelt song no one asked for.

Pro Tip: If you pass out somewhere inconvenient—like the cake table—*it's not your fault.*

5. Start Drama for No Reason

A wedding is the perfect place to stir the pot.

- Whisper to guests, "Wow, do you think they'll actually last?"
- Accidentally-on-purpose bring up family feuds that have been buried for years.
- If you catch the bridal bouquet, glare at your date and say, "So, what are we waiting for?"—especially if you've only been dating for a few months.

7. Hijack the Photographer

Wedding photographers are there to capture memories—your memories.

- Demand a full-on photo shoot of yourself.
- Photobomb every romantic picture.
- If the bride and groom try to take a private photo, casually stand behind them, holding a drink and grinning like a maniac.

Pro Tip: Make sure you're front and center in every group shot, even ones you weren't invited into.

8. Make a Scene During the Ceremony

The ceremony is a sacred moment. Time to ruin it.

- Loudly whisper, "Is it just me, or is this taking forever?"
- Answer *any* question the officiant asks with "I object!" (Even if you're joking, the tension will be palpable.)
- If kids are in the wedding party, compete for attention—fake trip down the aisle, drop something loudly, or *dramatically sigh* during vows.

9. Steal the Spotlight

At the end of the day, why should anyone else get the spotlight?

- Announce your own engagement right before dinner.
- Show up with a surprise plus-one who wasn't invited.

- Complain that the food, venue, or dress code wasn't up to *your* standards.

Weddings are meant to be joyful, but why let them be stress-free? By following this guide, you can ensure that the happy couple will always remember *your* presence—whether they want to or not.

And hey, if they don't invite you to the next wedding, that just means you did your job right.

30
MASTERING DISENGAGED BODY LANGUAGE

Body language is a powerful tool for communication—but why use it to show engagement when you can do the exact opposite? Instead of signaling that you're attentive, interested, or invested in a conversation, let your body language broadcast apathy, distraction, and mild disdain. This chapter will teach you how to ruin interactions without saying a word by perfecting disengaged body language.

Step 1: Avoid Eye Contact (and Overdo It When You Make It)

Eye contact is a surefire way to show you're paying attention, so naturally, you'll want to avoid it as much as possible. Instead, look at anything but the speaker: your phone, the ceiling, or a fascinating spot on the floor. If you do make eye contact, hold it for just a second too long before abruptly looking away—enough to make it awkward but not enough to seem intentional.

Example:

Them: "I've been feeling really stressed lately."

You: *glance at your watch* "Mmm, yeah, that's tough."

Pro Tip: Occasionally nod absentmindedly while staring off into the distance. This creates the illusion of politeness without actual engagement.

Step 2: Cross Your Arms and Lean Back

Nothing says "I'm not interested" like closed-off body language. Cross your arms tightly, lean back in your chair, and angle your body slightly away from the person speaking. These subtle cues make it clear that you're mentally checked out.

Example:

Them: "So, I've been working on this new project…"

You: *cross arms, lean back, and glance at your phone*

Pro Tip: Combine crossed arms with a raised eyebrow or a skeptical expression to exude an air of judgment or indifference.

Step 3: Fidget Constantly

Engaged listeners appear calm and focused, so fidgeting is your go-to move to disrupt that vibe. Tap your foot, drum your fingers, or adjust your clothing unnecessarily. If you have a pen, click it repeatedly. These subtle distractions will make the speaker feel like they're competing for your attention.

Example:

Them: "It was a really emotional moment for me."

You: *tap your pen against the table* "Uh-huh, totally."

Pro Tip: Pretend to suddenly notice something on your shoe and start fiddling with it mid-conversation.

Step 4: Face Away from the Speaker

Orientation matters. Instead of facing the person you're speaking with, angle your body slightly away from them. This creates a physical barrier that signals, "I'd rather be anywhere else."

Example:

Them: "I'm so glad we could catch up today."

You: *half-turn toward them while glancing out the window* "Yeah, me too."

Pro Tip: If seated, shift your chair just enough to make them feel like they're talking to your side profile.

Step 5: Show Disinterest Through Facial Expressions

Engaged listeners mirror emotions and maintain an open, welcoming expression. Instead, opt for a blank stare, an exaggerated yawn, or a subtle eye roll. If they share something exciting, respond with a flat, "Oh, cool," while maintaining a neutral face.

Example:

Them: "I just got promoted at work!"

You: *raise one eyebrow and shrug* "Nice."

Pro Tip: If you're feeling extra bold, check your nails or glance at your phone while they're talking.

Step 6: Interrupt or Zone Out

One of the easiest ways to show disengagement is to either cut them off mid-sentence or let your mind wander so far that you clearly have no idea what they just said.

Example:

Them: "And that's when I realized I..."

You: "Oh, hold on, did you see that email about the sale?"

Alternatively, let them finish their thought, pause, and then say, "Wait, sorry, what were you talking about again?"

Pro Tip: If they ask, "Are you listening?" respond with, "Yeah, yeah, totally," while clearly not listening.

Reflection Exercise:

Think about your most recent conversation. Did you:

1. Maintain eye contact, lean in, and show genuine interest?
2. Actively listen but occasionally get distracted?
3. Cross your arms, fidget, and stare into the void while they spoke?

If you answered 3, pat yourself on the back! You're nailing the art of disengaged body language.

Body language speaks louder than words, and when used incorrectly (or deliberately poorly), it can make even the most engaging conversation feel like a chore. By following these steps, you'll ensure that every interaction leaves the other person feeling unheard, undervalued, and slightly annoyed. After all, why bother with active listening when you can silently sabotage the vibe?

31

HOW TO MAKE A TERRIBLE FIRST IMPRESSION

First impressions are everything... if you care about people liking you. But if your goal is to repel, irritate, or confuse, why not make your first impression unforgettable for all the wrong reasons? In this chapter, we'll explore the art of making an entrance that ensures people remember you—and avoid you—forever.

Step 1: Arrive Late (or Way Too Early)

Show up either fashionably late or embarrassingly early, depending on how uncomfortable you want to make everyone. Arriving late shows that you're too important to care about their time, while showing up early ensures the host scrambles to accommodate you.

Example:

- Late arrival: "Oh, is this thing still going? I almost didn't make it... traffic was insane."

- Early arrival: "Oh, you're still setting up? Don't mind me... I'll just hang out in the corner."

Step 2: Skip the Pleasantries

Why waste time with polite greetings when you can jump straight into something awkward or inappropriate? Skip the handshakes and small talk and go for comments that catch people off guard.

Example:

- "Wow, your profile picture doesn't do you justice."
- "I'm terrible with names, so don't expect me to remember yours."

Pro Tip: If someone offers a polite smile, counter with a deadpan expression or an exaggerated frown to keep them guessing.

Step 3: Steal the Show

First impressions should be a showcase of how amazing you are… and nothing else. Interrupt conversations, talk over people, and steer every topic back to your own experiences.

Example:

- Them: "I just got back from a trip to Europe."
- You: "Oh, Europe? I've been there three times. Did you visit [insert place]? That's the best spot. Let me tell you about my time there."

Pro Tip: Bragging works best when it's irrelevant. Even if the conversation is about someone else's promotion, casually drop, "That reminds me of the time I got a raise for being so awesome."

Step 4: Ignore Names and Details

Remembering someone's name or what they just said is a rookie move. Instead, make it clear that you're not invested enough to care.

Example:

Them: "Hi, I'm Sarah."

You: "Oh, cool. So, what do you do… Susan?"

If they correct you, brush it off with, "I'm terrible with names… but I'll try to remember."

Step 5: Dominate the Conversation

First impressions aren't about listening, they're about making yourself heard. Interrupt frequently, dismiss others' points, and steer the discussion toward topics you're interested in.

Example:

Them: "I've been working on this new project…"

You: "Oh, that reminds me of something way more interesting… let me tell you about it."

If someone tries to contribute, talk louder or wave them off with a dismissive, "Hold on, I'm not finished."

Pro Tip: Overuse phrases like, "Let's get back to what I was saying…" to keep the spotlight on you.

Step 6: Exude Overconfidence

Confidence is attractive, but overconfidence is unforgettable. Strut into the room as if you own it and sprinkle your conversations with exaggerations about your achievements.

Example:

- "Yeah, I've pretty much mastered that skill. People say I'm a natural genius."
- "This event is great, but honestly, I've been to way better ones."

Pro Tip: Pair your overconfidence with a touch of condescension. Say things like, "Don't worry, you'll get there someday," or "It's not as hard as people make it out to be."

Reflection Exercise:

Think about your most recent first impression. Did you:

1. Show up on time, engage politely, and listen actively?
2. Make a few awkward jokes but ultimately get along?
3. Arrive late, dominate the conversation, and forget everyone's names?

If you answered 3, you are probably already great at terrible first impressions.

First impressions don't have to be about charm, connection, or building rapport. Sometimes, the best way to stand out is to do everything wrong. By following these steps, you'll leave an impression so strong that people won't forget you—even if they want to.

32

HOW TO BE A SPECTACULARLY INEFFECTIVE LEADER

Leadership is about inspiring others, fostering teamwork, and earning respect... unless your goal is to create chaos and resentment. Why lead effectively when you can undermine morale, derail progress, and leave everyone questioning your abilities? In this chapter, we'll explore all the ways to be a spectacularly ineffective leader, ensuring your team remembers you—just not for the right reasons.

Step 1: Micromanage Everything

A good leader delegates, but an ineffective one clutches every tiny detail with an iron grip. Show your team you don't trust them by hovering over their shoulders, nitpicking their work, and demanding updates every five minutes.

Example:

- "Let me watch you type that email—no, wait, change that word... actually, rewrite the whole opening sentence."

Make them feel like they can't write even a sentence without your oversight.

Pro Tip: Set unrealistic deadlines and check in constantly to ensure they feel overwhelmed and underappreciated.

Step 2: Avoid Taking Responsibility

When things go wrong (and they will, under your leadership), make sure to shift the blame onto others. Never admit fault or acknowledge mistakes—that's for effective leaders.

<u>Example:</u>

- "I don't know how this happened, but clearly, someone dropped the ball."
- "If only my team had followed my instructions properly, we wouldn't be in this mess."

Pro Tip: Pair your blame-shifting with vague solutions that put the burden back on your team. Say things like, "Let's all try to be better next time," without offering any actionable guidance.

Step 3: Play Favorites

Nothing kills team cohesion like blatant favoritism. Make it clear that some people's ideas, contributions, and time are more valuable than others. Bonus points if your favorites are less competent than the other colleagues.

<u>Example:</u>

- Always ask the same person for their opinion in meetings while ignoring everyone else.

- Assign the easiest tasks to your favorite team members and the most challenging ones to the people you dislike.

Pro Tip: Publicly praise your favorites, even when they don't deserve it. This will foster resentment and division among the rest of the team.

Step 4: Communicate Poorly (or Not at All)

Effective leaders are clear and transparent, but you're here to sow confusion. Give vague instructions, change priorities without warning, and hold meetings that accomplish nothing.

Example:

- "Just get it done. You know what I mean, right?"
- "I'll let you know the details later… but just start working on it for now."

Pro Tip: If someone asks for clarification, respond with, "Figure it out. That's why I hired you."

Step 5: Lead by Fear, Not Respect

An ineffective leader knows the power of intimidation. Use your authority to make people feel small, anxious, and expendable. This way, they'll focus more on avoiding your wrath than on doing good work.

Example:

- "If this project fails, it's your job on the line, not mine."

Pro Tip: Publicly criticize team members for mistakes, no matter how minor. This will ensure a culture of fear and low morale.

Step 6: Take All the Credit, Share All the Blame

When your team achieves something great, make sure everyone knows it was because of your brilliant leadership. Conversely, when something goes wrong, make sure the blame is widely distributed (except to you, of course).

Example:

- "This success wouldn't have been possible without my vision and guidance."
- "We all need to reflect on how we let this failure happen."

Pro Tip: When presenting team achievements to higher-ups, minimize individual contributions. Say, "We worked hard on this," while subtly implying it was mostly you.

Reflection Exercise:

Think about your leadership style. Do you:

1. Empower and inspire your team to do their best?
2. Occasionally stumble but ultimately have your teams respect?
3. Micromanage, blame others, and take credit for everything?

If you answered 3, a job well executed! You're already honing the skill of ineffective leadership.

Being an effective leader is overhyped. By following these steps, you can create an environment of chaos, resentment, and distrust. Sure, your team might not thrive… but at least you'll always be in control (or at least look like you are). After all, who needs success when you can have power?

33

HOW TO ROPE SOMEONE INTO DOING SOMETHING (THEY NEVER WANTED TO DO)

So, you want someone to participate in an activity they never agreed to? Maybe it's a couples' dance class, a grueling hike at sunrise, or a pottery workshop because *"it'll be fun, I swear!"*—even though they *explicitly* said they had zero interest in doing it. The key here is to eliminate their ability to say no by using guilt, obligation, and just enough enthusiasm to make them question their own feelings.

Step 1: Act Like It Was Already Decided

Never ask if they want to do something—just tell them it's happening. The trick is to present it like a done deal rather than an option.

Example:

- "Okay, so we're all doing a 5K fun run next weekend! I already signed us up—it's gonna be amazing!"
- "I put your name down for the work committee, so you're on the email list now!"

How This Works:

The shock of being blindsided will override their ability to immediately protest, buying you valuable time to reinforce your plan.

Step 2: Use the "I Did This for YOU" Tactic

If they seem hesitant, flip the script so that saying no makes them feel like an ungrateful monster.

Example:

- "But I already bought you yoga pants for the class! You *have* to come now!"
- "I told everyone you were coming! If you don't, I'll look bad…"
- "I spent so much time researching this—just give it a try!"

How This Works:

Instead of it being about what *they* want, it's suddenly about your effort, generosity, and fragile emotional state. A true guilt masterpiece.

Step 3: Downplay the Commitment *(aka the "It's No Big Deal" Lie)*

If they're still resisting, make it sound like the easiest thing in the world.

Example:

- "It's literally just an hour. ONE hour. You spend more time scrolling on your phone."
- "Just try it once! If you hate it, you never have to do it again." (Spoiler: They'll never hear the end of it.)
- "You don't even have to be good at it, just show up!"

How This Works:

Minimizing the effort makes their objections seem dramatic and irrational, forcing them to cave just to avoid looking difficult.

Step 4: Lock in the Commitment Publicly

Saying no to you is one thing, but saying no in front of a crowd of witnesses? That's next-level social pressure.

Example:

- *At a group dinner:* "Oh, we're all doing karaoke after this! Right, [Victim's Name]?"
- *In a group chat:* "We're officially all signed up for hot yoga on Sunday!! Can't wait!!"
- *With mutual friends:* "I got us theater tickets!! Oh… you're busy? But I already told everyone you were coming…"

How This Works:

They now have an audience, meaning their refusal comes with public disappointment and awkwardness. Beautiful.

Step 5: The Non-Refundable Trap

If all else fails, hit them with the financial investment tactic—aka "I already paid for it."

Example:

- "I bought the class pass, so you HAVE to come."
- "It was a group rate so I already covered you."
- "I booked the Airbnb and put you in the room with me!"

How This Works:

The sunk-cost fallacy will work in your favor—because who wants to waste money? Definitely not them.

Reflection Exercise:

Think about your social life. Do you:

1. Respect people's boundaries and ask before committing them to things?

2. Occasionally pressure friends into plans but accept a "no" when you hear it?

3. Sign people up for things without asking, buy them "guilt gifts," and act shocked when they try to back out?

If you answered 3, you're the reason your friends now triple-check texts before replying. Keep it up, and soon they'll start *accidentally* missing your messages altogether

---

By following these steps, you'll effortlessly trap someone into an activity they never wanted to do—and the best part? They'll feel too guilty to back out.

And if they *actually* enjoy it?
Well, then you get to say, "*See?* I told you so."

34

THE ART OF NEVER LETTING THEM ESCAPE

Have you ever noticed when people are eager to leave, slip out of a social event or running late to be somewhere? Well, you're not here to make it easy for them. Instead, hijack their attempt to exit while continuing the conversation into a trap they simply can't wiggle out of. Whether they're trying to hang up or head home, your job is to prolong the interaction until they're practically begging to leave. Welcome to the art of never letting them escape.

Step 1: Keep the Conversation Looping

Nothing says "You're not free yet" like recycling the same topics endlessly or introducing new ones when they think you're about to wrap things up.

Example (Phone Call):

Them: "Okay, I really must go—"

You: "Oh, but did I tell you about the time my coworker brought a raccoon to the office? I swear, it'll be quick…"

Resist any attempts at a polite exit. Each time they utter a goodbye or show a sign of leaving, latch onto a new topic, question, or random factoid that can't possibly wait.

Pro Tip: Suddenly remember "one last thing," and then keep remembering more last things. This should happen at least three or four times.

Step 2: Ignore All Social Cues

Body language and subtle hints mean nothing to you. Yawning, glancing at the door, or even physically getting up to leave is no reason to end the conversation.

<u>*Example*</u>:

Them: *Gathers coat, checks the time*

You: "Wait, before you go, I just have to tell you about this amazing documentary I saw last year. You love documentaries, right?"

If they continue moving, step in front of them or place a gentle hand on their shoulder to force continued engagement.

Pro Tip: If they mention needing the bathroom, respond with, "Great! Let's walk and talk. I'll catch you up on the way!"

Step 3: Use Guilt to Bind Them

When someone insists they must go, turn up the emotional pressure. Make them feel like leaving early is a personal slight against you.

<u>*Example*</u>:

- "Oh, you're leaving already? I guess my stories aren't interesting enough for you…"
- "Damn, I only wanted five more minutes of your time."

Lace your words with disappointment, ensuring they feel guilty enough to hang around a while longer. The more uncomfortable they become, the more successful you are.

Pro Tip: If they try to set a boundary, respond with, "I just feel like you're shutting me out... but it's fine, I'll manage." Nothing hooks them faster than perceived emotional damage.

Step 4: Physical Barriers (in Moderation)

If they truly attempt to flee a social event or your home, you might need more direct methods. Position yourself between them and the exit or move personal belongings they need—like keys or a coat—away from the door.

Example:

- Casually relocate their coat to a different room. "Oh, I hung it up upstairs to dry! Let me get that after I finish telling you about my new hobby."

Make them chase their belongings through your labyrinth of conversation. By the time they reclaim their stuff, you'll have at least two more topics to discuss.

Pro Tip: Avoid anything too blatantly aggressive—like locking doors—unless you want them to call the police. The idea is to keep them 'voluntarily' trapped in conversation.

Reflection Exercise:

Ask yourself:

1. Have you ever noticed someone inching away as you talk?

2. Do people often say, "I've got to run," only for you to ignore it?

3. Does your chatter drive them to invent excuses like "My pet fish needs me"?

If you answered "Yes" to any of these, Bravo! You're already a veteran at keeping people longer than they intend.

Trapping someone in an endless conversation isn't just about words, it's about sensing their desperation to leave and powering through anyway. Master these techniques, and you'll ensure nobody escapes your orbit without a struggle. After all, why let them depart politely when you can savor every second of forced social interaction?

Did you know?

If you stand just slightly too close, people are 64% less likely to tell you they have to leave because they're too afraid to move?

35

HOW TO RUIN BATHROOM ETIQUETTE

Bathrooms are meant to be shared spaces of peace, quiet, and cleanliness. Naturally, this makes them a perfect target for chaos and annoyance. Whether you're among friends, family, or coworkers, a few strategic moves can ensure you'll never be invited to use the bathroom again—if not the house altogether. Here are the ultimate ways to becoming a bathroom bandit and leave a lasting impression (for better or worse).

---

1. Leave the Toilet Seat Up

- For those sharing a bathroom with friends, family, or coworkers, this classic move never fails to annoy. Make sure to leave the seat—and maybe even the lid—up every time you go.

- Extra points if someone's first discovery of this is in the middle of the night.

Pro Tip: Make it seem intentional by saying, "I thought you'd appreciate having options!"

2. The Empty Roll Trick

- Always finish the last square of toilet paper but *never* replace the roll. Let others deal with the consequences of your lack of foresight.

- Bonus move: hide the rest of the spare toilet rolls to be sure to leave them in a pickle.

Pro Tip: Blame the next person with, "Oh, I thought you liked bringing your own roll."

3. Half-Flushing or Not Flushing at All

- Why waste water when you can leave a surprise for the next person? Whether it's a half-flush that doesn't quite get the job done or no flush at all, this move guarantees a memorable reaction.

Pro Tip: When confronted, claim you're "saving the planet—one flush at a time."

4. Splash Zone

- Wash your hands (good start!) but leave water everywhere: the sink, the counter, and maybe even the mirror. Bonus: Leave soap residue to add a slimy touch.

Pro Tip: Declare, "That's just how I show I care—it's my signature splash!"

5. Towel Terror

- Use the bathroom towel and leave it sopping wet, crumpled in a heap, or—better yet—on the floor. For extra fun, use a decorative hand towel that's clearly *for show*.

Pro Tip: Say, "I thought it was meant to be used! Isn't that the point?"

6. Hog the Bathroom

- Spend an unreasonable amount of time in the bathroom for something mundane. Check your phone, do your makeup, or just linger unnecessarily.
- Bonus Move: Do this when you know someone's waiting urgently outside.

Pro Tip: When they knock, yell, "This is *me* time—you'll survive!"

7. Leave *Personal Touches* Everywhere

- Scatter your belongings across every available surface. Razor on the sink? Check. Hairbrush on the counter? Double-check. Toothpaste lid? Missing.

Pro Tip: When they complain, say, "Oh, I thought it added character to the room!"

8. *Forget* to Ventilate

- After doing your business, skip turning on the fan or cracking the window. For extra impact, leave the door shut to trap the smell and let it marinate a little more.

Pro Tip: If they complain about the smell, tell them, "I don't know what you're talking about, it smells like roses!"

9. Leave *Mystery Stains*

Nothing says "I was here" quite like an unexplained splatter on the toilet seat, a white towel, sink, or—if you're feeling particularly diabolical—the wall. Keep it vague, keep it ominous, and most importantly, never clean it up.

Pro Tip: Shrug and say, "Huh, weird. That was definitely there before I came in."

Bathrooms are sacred spaces, but that doesn't mean they can't be the scene of glorious sabotage. By following these tips, you can ensure that every visit you make to a shared bathroom is remembered—and not in a good way. Just be prepared for awkward confrontations… or a sternly worded group chat message.

36

THE HIGH-MAINTENANCE SICK PERSON

Being sick is tough—but why suffer in silence when you can make everyone else suffer with you? Whether it's a mild cold or a minor headache, your job isn't just to recover—it's to ensure that everyone in your life feels your misery on a deeply personal level. After all, what's the point of being sick if you don't get attention for it?

Step 1: Announce Your Illness Loudly and Frequently

If you don't regularly remind people that you're sick, are you even sick at all? Make sure your suffering is always the number one conversation topic.

Example:

- "I think I have the worst cold in human history."
- "I barely slept last night. My throat feels like sandpaper. Do you think it's strep?"
- "Ugh, I feel so awful… But I'm here anyway! No one say I don't make sacrifices."

Pro Tip: Show up to work or social events so everyone can witness your suffering in real-time, even when no one wants to be around whatever illness you're carrying. Bonus points if you manage to get someone else sick—because misery loves company.

Step 2: Turn Every Interaction into a Plea for Sympathy

It's not enough for people to know you're sick—they need to suffer alongside you. Make sure they understand just how brave and tragic your situation is.

How to Do It:

- Sigh dramatically whenever someone asks how you're feeling.
- Make weak, pathetic noises as you slowly lower yourself into chairs.
- Respond to simple requests with, "I guess I'll try... even though I feel like death."

Pro Tip: If someone else mentions they're sick, immediately one-up their suffering. "Oh, you have a sore throat? That's nothing! I think my lungs are collapsing."

Step 3: Refuse to Take Basic Care of Yourself

Could you drink water, rest, and take some medicine? Of course! But that would ruin the whole experience of making everyone else responsible for your well-being.

What to Do Instead:

- Refuse to do anything to get better and then complain that nothing is helping.
- Insist on showing up to work, social events, or family gatherings just to remind everyone how miserable you are.
- Moan about how exhausted you are while staying up until 2 AM watching Netflix.

Pro Tip: If someone suggests a remedy, shoot it down immediately. "Oh, vitamin C? No, I think my immune system is beyond saving."

Step 4: Make Everyone Else's Life Harder

If you're suffering, then it's only fair that others suffer too. Take every possible opportunity to be inconvenient and needy.

Key Techniques:

- Text your friends at all hours for moral support. Bonus points if you send pictures of your mucus filled tissues.
- Demand endless favors: "Can you grab me soup? But not just any soup—the one from that place across town."
- Use your sickness as an excuse for everything. Missed a deadline? Can't help with chores? Accidentally insulted someone? Just blame it on the fever.

Pro Tip: If someone doesn't immediately rush to help you, act deeply wounded. A well-placed, "Wow, I guess I know where I stand now," should do the trick.

Step 5: Return to Normal—But Keep the Drama Alive

Once you recover, don't just move on quietly, make sure everyone remembers your heroic battle.

How to Do It:

- Mention your near-death experience at least twice a day for the next two weeks.
- Refer to it as "The Worst Sickness I've Ever Had" (even if it was just a mild cold).
- Milk the last bit of sympathy for as long as humanly possible.

Pro Tip: Casually bring up your *weakened immune system* to get out of things you don't want to do. "Ugh, I'd totally help move your furniture, but I'm still recovering."

If you have followed these steps or already find yourself doing most of them, well done! You've successfully made your illness everyone else's problem. Now, go forth and weaponize that cough—after all, a little dramatic flair never hurt anyone (except the people stuck dealing with you).

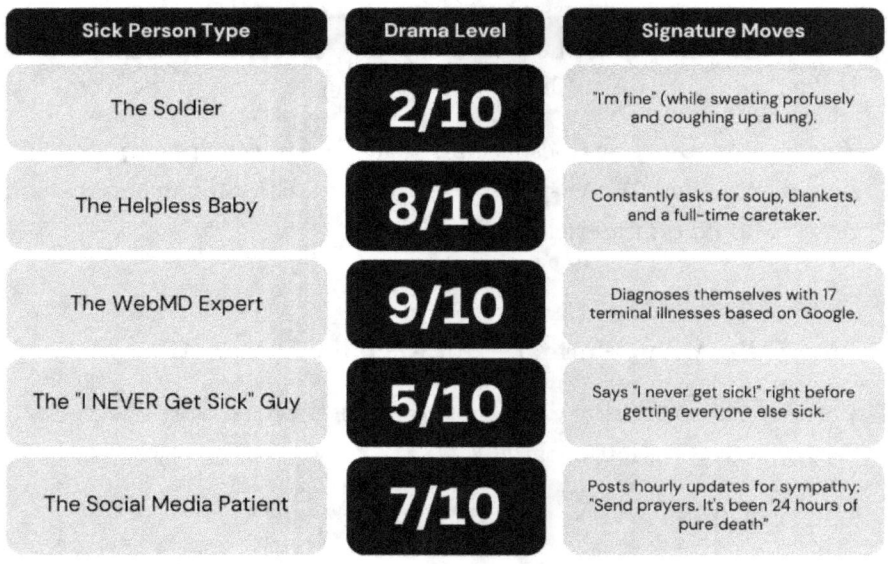

37

THE COUPLE THAT SHOULD HAVE BROKEN UP AGES AGO

Every friend group has one. That couple that fights so often, so publicly, and so dramatically that everyone else actively dreads being around them. Whether it's their passive-aggressive digs, their full-blown screaming matches at dinner, or the unbearable tension they bring to every social event, these two have mastered the art of making everyone deeply uncomfortable.

Step 1: Argue in Public at Every Opportunity

Nothing keeps a relationship alive like a good, loud, awkward fight in front of friends and strangers alike. Why wait until you're alone when you can pull everyone into your emotional battlefield?

Common Public Fight Starters:

- "Wow, I love how you just ignore me in front of our friends."
- "Are you seriously bringing THAT up again?"
- "Maybe if you actually listened to me for once…"

Pro Tip: The key is timing. Start a tense argument right before food arrives so everyone gets to experience the meal alongside your relationship turmoil.

Step 2: Put Your Friends in the Middle

It's not enough to fight in front of people—you need to drag them into it. Make sure your friends are forced to pick sides, give advice, or mediate disputes they never wanted to be part of.

<u>*Example*</u>:

- Ask your friend: "Do you think I'm being unreasonable?" (There is no safe answer.)
- Say things like: "Can you tell them how wrong they are?" while your partner glares at them.
- Force people to sit between you when you're clearly mid-fight.

Pro Tip: If a friend tries to stay neutral, act betrayed. "Wow, I thought you had my back."

Step 3: Weaponize Social Media

Who needs couples therapy when you have cryptic Instagram stories and passive-aggressive Facebook posts?

<u>Key Strategies:</u>

- Post a black screen with the text "Some people just don't appreciate what they have…"
- Delete and re-add your relationship status every few months.
- Post a smiling couple's selfie with a suspiciously defensive caption like "Through thick and thin" after a public screaming match.

Pro Tip: Nothing says healthy relationship like blocking and unblocking each other every other week.

Step 4: Break Up Constantly—But Never for Good

Why commit to an actual breakup when you can keep your friends on a never-ending emotional rollercoaster?

Example:

- Announce your breakup in the group chat with dramatic details.
- Show up back together the next day like nothing happened.
- Expect your friends to remember and respect every temporary breakup rule (e.g., "Don't invite them if I'm there.").

Pro Tip: Use phrases like "We're just working through things" even though nothing ever changes.

Step 5: Make Every Event About Your Dysfunction

Whether it's a party, wedding, or simple dinner, make sure your ongoing disaster of a relationship takes center stage.

Example:

- Fight loudly at someone else's birthday party.
- Get jealous over small, meaningless interactions ("Oh, so you liked their Instagram post but not mine?").
- Have a dramatic public breakup during a night out, only to be back together before the Uber ride home.

Pro Tip: If anyone tries to enjoy themselves despite your mess, shoot them a look like they aren't being supportive enough.

Reflection Exercise:

Think about your relationship. Do you:

1. Communicate openly and respectfully, solving problems without making everyone else uncomfortable?

2. Have occasional rough patches but overall maintain a healthy and functional relationship?

3. Turn every group outing into a battleground, weaponize social media, and make your friends pick sides?

If you answered 3, you and your partner are the stars of the show—whether anyone wants to watch or not. Keep up the drama, and soon your friends will start mysteriously having *other plans* whenever you invite them out.

If your goal is to make everyone around you wish they had left five minutes earlier, congratulations! Your relationship is the perfect lesson in what not to do. Whether you stay together out of pure stubbornness or simply to keep ruining brunches, one thing is for sure: no one enjoys being around you two.

But hey, at least you have each other. Right? (For now.)

38

HOW TO MAKE EVERY MEAL UNBEARABLE

Dining with others is a sacred ritual of bonding, laughter, and shared experiences—unless, of course, you make it a complete nightmare for everyone involved. Whether you're at a fine-dining establishment, a family dinner, or just a casual meal with friends, follow these steps to ensure nobody ever invites you out again.

Step 1: Chew Like a Farm Animal

Why enjoy your food quietly when you can make every bite a performance? The louder, the better.

Example:

- Smack your lips with exaggerated enthusiasm.
- Chew with your mouth wide open, ensuring maximum visibility of your food.
- Add some commentary while chewing—everyone loves hearing a sentence interrupted by the wet, sloshing sound of half-masticated spaghetti.

Pro Tip: If someone gives you a disgusted look, double down by making eye contact while loudly crunching a chip.

Step 2: Talk With Your Mouth Full

A conversation isn't complete unless people can see exactly what you're saying—literally.

Key Moves:

- Start an animated discussion just as you take a massive bite.
- Send tiny bits of food flying with each syllable.
- Occasionally pause mid-sentence to fish something out of your teeth—with your fingers, of course.

Pro Tip: If someone politely asks you to finish chewing before speaking, look deeply offended and say, "Wow, I didn't realize we were in a finishing school."

Step 3: Treat the Table Like Your Personal Napkin

Why use an actual napkin when your sleeve, the tablecloth, or your own face will do just fine?

Essential Techniques:

- Wipe your hands on whatever is closest—even if it's your friend's sleeve.
- Lick your fingers dramatically after eating something messy.
- Blow your nose into your napkin mid-meal, then place it back on the table like nothing happened.

Pro Tip: Bonus points if you leave mysterious grease stains on everything you touch.

Step 4: Make Eating as Disruptive as Possible

There's no such thing as too much table noise—so embrace every sound and movement like a true chaos agent.

Disruptive Dining Strategies:

- Clank your utensils against the plate as loudly as possible.
- Scrape your fork across your teeth while taking a bite.
- Stir your soup aggressively so it splashes everywhere.
- Slurp every liquid like it's your final meal on Earth.

Pro Tip: If you're drinking something carbonated, time your burps for maximum impact—preferably mid-conversation.

Step 5: Show No Regard for Personal Space

Dining is a communal experience, so why not invade everyone else's space while you're at it?

Ways to Make It Awkward:

- Reach across the table without warning, knocking over glasses and elbows in the process.
- Steal food off someone's plate while making intense eye contact.
- Eat way too close to your neighbor, breathing audibly between bites.

Pro Tip: If someone asks for some space, scoot closer instead and whisper, "Sharing is caring."

Step 6: Ignore Basic Hygiene

If you want to truly ruin a meal, disregard all common decency when it comes to hygiene.

Things to Avoid (But You Won't):

- Cough directly over the table—bonus points if you don't cover your mouth.
- Pick food out of your teeth and flick it away casually.
- Drop food on the table and eat it anyway without hesitation.
- Scratch your armpits right before reaching for the breadbasket.

Pro Tip: If someone side-eyes your unsanitary habits, act confused and say, "Oh, sorry, I didn't realize we were in the presence of royalty."

By following these simple steps, you can ensure that every meal is an unbearable ordeal for those around you. Whether it's your unapologetic mouth sounds, intrusive behavior, or complete disregard for hygiene, your dining presence will be one to remember—for all the wrong reasons. So go forth, chew loudly, and make sure that no dinner party ever feels peaceful again.

39

ARE YOU A FRIEND-LOSING CHAMPION?

Answer these questions to find out if you've mastered the fine art of losing friends and pissing people off. Choose the answer that best describes you for each scenario.

---

1. A friend is telling a story during dinner. What do you do?

- A) Listen intently and ask follow-up questions.
- B) Nod along but keep checking your phone.
- C) Interrupt with, "Oh, that reminds me of the time I…" and take over the conversation.

2. How do you handle splitting the check after a group dinner?

- A) Suggest dividing it evenly and pay your share promptly.
- B) Fumble for your wallet but pay when pressed.
- C) Pretend you left your wallet at home and say, "Can someone cover me this time?"

3. Your coworker gets promoted. How do you react?

- A) Congratulate them and celebrate their success.
- B) Say, "Must be nice," and walk away.
- C) Post on social media: "Some people have all the luck…"

4. How do you behave at game night?

- A) Play fairly and cheer for others.
- B) Get a little competitive but still have fun.
- C) Accuse everyone of cheating and rage-quit when you lose.

5. How do you handle eating in a social situation?

- A) Use a napkin, chew quietly, and make sure to respect personal space.
- B) Occasionally forget table manners but at least make an effort to be decent.
- C) Smack your lips, chew loudly, steal bites from others' plates, and slurp your drink as loudly as possible.

6. A friend invites you to a movie night. What's your strategy?

- A) Show up on time, bring snacks, and enjoy the film.
- B) Chat a little during the movie but keep it light.
- C) Critique every plot hole, spoil the ending, and argue about their favorite scenes.

7. How do you approach being a guest at someone's house?

- A) Respect their space and clean up after yourself.
- B) Stay an extra day or two but offer to help out.
- C) Borrow their things without asking, leave dirty dishes everywhere, and call it "living authentically."

8. When you're leading a project, how do you act?

- A) Delegate tasks and support your team.
- B) Take on most of the work yourself but get overwhelmed.
- C) Micromanage every detail and take all the credit.

9. Someone shares good news with you. How do you respond?

- A) Celebrate with genuine enthusiasm.
- B) Say, "That's great for you," but change the subject quickly.
- C) Talk about how hard things have been for you lately to shift the focus back to yourself.

10. How do you handle honesty?

- A) Offer thoughtful feedback when asked.
- B) Blurt out your thoughts but apologize if they're hurtful.
- C) Say things like, "I'm just being real," after delivering brutal, unfiltered opinions.

Scoring:

- For every A: 1 point
- For every B: 2 points
- For every C: 3 points

Results:

- **10-15 Points:** Friendship goals! You're a supportive and likable person (maybe pass this book along to someone who needs it more).
- **16-25 Points:** You've got some chaotic tendencies, but there's still hope for you. Pick your battles wisely!
- **26-30 Points:** You've earned your bragging rights! You're a certified friend-losing pro. Use your skills responsibly... or not.

40

THE SOCIAL SABOTEUR AWARDS CEREMONY

It's time to introduce you to the *Social Saboteur Awards Ceremony*, where we celebrate the best (or worst) in obnoxious, cringe-worthy, and downright hilarious social behaviors. This is your moment to shine! Because at the end of the day, we all deserve recognition for our contributions to the chaos.

Take a moment to reflect. Which award feels like it was made for you? Maybe more than one? Better yet, pass this list around to your friends and coworkers and let them vote on which category fits you best— or, for extra fun, assign awards to them. Just be ready for some awkward laughter (and maybe a little passive-aggressive backlash).

---

1. Most Likely to Forget Their Wallet Award

- Do you frequently *accidentally* leave your wallet at home? If so, this award is for you! Your unparalleled ability to dodge the bill ensures you never leave a meal hungry—or broke.

2. Best Use of Passive Aggression Award

- Is your go-to communication style a mix of sarcasm and thinly veiled hostility? Do you prefer phrases like, "Oh, don't worry, I didn't expect much anyway," or leave post-it notes in shared spaces instead of speaking up? Congratulations—you've perfected the art of irritation through subtlety.

3. The Houdini Award for Ghosting

- This one goes to the person who vanishes from group chats, leaves texts unanswered for weeks, and reappears with a casual, "Hey, what's up?" as if nothing happened. If your talent lies in making people question whether you're still alive, this is your category.

4. The One-Upper Extraordinaire Award

- If you can't resist turning someone else's accomplishment into an opportunity to share your bigger, better, and totally-not-exaggerated story, this award belongs to you. Bonus points if you've ever one-upped someone's vacation with an imaginary trip to the moon.

5. Lifetime Achievement in Gossip

- For the person who knows everyone's business—whether it's true or not. You don't just spread information; you enhance it for dramatic effect. If your motto is "I'm just telling you what I heard," this award goes to you.

6. The Fashionably Late Award

- Do you consistently show up late to every event, claiming it's part of your "personal brand"? This award celebrates your ability to make others wait, ensuring your entrance is as disruptive as it is memorable.

7. The Boundary Breaker Award

- Do you overshare, overstep, or invite yourself to other people's plans uninvited? If you've ever borrowed something and forgotten to return it—or conveniently forgot to ask in the first place—you might just be this year's winner.

8. The Group Photo Menace Award

- This one's for the person who insists on retaking group photos until they look perfect—regardless of how everyone else appears. Bonus points if you post a picture where you look great, but everyone else's eyes are closed.

9. The Overstaying Guest Award

- Are you the last one to leave every party, even after the host has started cleaning up? If you've ever helped yourself to leftovers without asking or suggested "one more drink" when everyone else is clearly done, this award has your name on it.

10. The Bathroom Bandit Award

- Do you leave empty toilet paper rolls without replacing them? Maybe you mysteriously *forget* to flush or leave unidentifiable stains in the sink. If people enter the bathroom after you and immediately turn around in horror, congratulations—you're the undisputed champion of restroom sabotage.

Congratulations to all our winners—you've truly gone above and beyond in the fine art of social sabotage. Wear your award with pride… or shame. Either way, you've earned it.

41

REDEMPTION
(IN CASE YOU ACTUALLY WANT TO KEEP YOUR FRIENDS)

So, you've almost read the entire book, laughed (hopefully), maybe recognized a few of your own questionable habits or answered mostly Cs in the quiz, and are now wondering: "Wait, am I actually... like this?" First, take a moment to commend your self-awareness, not everyone will be able to recognise or admit to it. Second, if you suspect you might need to backtrack a bit—or at least disguise your worst impulses—this chapter is for you. Think of it as a crash course on how to reverse (or cleverly mask) all those friend-losing tactics we've covered. Here are a few ideas:

Step 1: Experiment with Genuine Listening (Just a Little)

You've spent countless pages ignoring, interrupting, and hijacking conversations. Maybe, just maybe, give genuine listening a shot. Make eye contact, nod occasionally, and resist the urge to cut them off with your own story.

Example:

Them: *Sharing a heartfelt concern*

You: *Actually, sit quietly for two whole minutes and respond with something empathetic, like,* "That sounds tough. Let me know if I can help."

Shocking, I know.

Pro Tip: If that feels too sincere, at least pretend to listen by repeating one relevant detail before pivoting back to yourself. Baby steps.

Step 2: Try a Random Act of Kindness (Nobody Has to Know Why)

From snatching the last donut to "forgetting" your wallet, you've mastered the art of taking. Maybe it's time to give something back—purely for shock value, of course.

<u>Example:</u>

- Offer to pay for the next coffee run (with actual money, not imaginary IOUs).
- Bring a small treat or helpful gadget to a coworker you've been tormenting.

Your goal here isn't permanent transformation—just enough benevolence to keep your social circle from mutiny.

Pro Tip: If you're worried about ruining your reputation, do it in secret. Pay for someone's meal anonymously so you can maintain plausible deniability.

Step 3: Consider Apologizing (the Real Kind, not "Sorry You Feel That Way")

Yes, apologies can be terrifying, especially after you've spent an entire book dodging responsibility. But a genuine apology can work wonders on friendships teetering on the edge.

Example:

- "I'm sorry I kept interrupting you. It was rude, and I'll try to do better."

Painful, right? But the payoff is worth it when you see their astonished faces.

Pro Tip: Keep it short, own your mistake, and don't add a "but" or deflection at the end. Quick, straightforward apologies are the hardest to argue with.

Step 4: Let Others Have Their Moment

Turning wins into your personal pity party has been a blast, but maybe it's time to let someone else have the spotlight. Offer genuine compliments and let them soak in the praise without sneaking in a backhanded dig.

Example:

Friend: "I just got a promotion!"

You: "That's amazing. You've worked really hard for it—I'm proud of you."

Take a second to bask in the uncomfortable feeling of sincerely celebrating someone else's success. You'll get used to it… eventually.

Step 5: Know When to Quit

Sometimes, the most revolutionary step is to stop a bad habit before it spirals out of control. If you catch yourself building drama or planning a petty comeback, pause and think, *Is this really worth the fallout?*

Example:

- About to ghost someone for weeks?
  Send a quick text: "Hey, life's hectic, but I'm good—how are you?"
- On the brink of sabotaging a game night?
  Breathe and let the dice rolls happen without accusations of cheating.

Every relationship you don't nuke is a small victory for decency.

Reflection Exercise:

Ask yourself:

- "Do I want to keep any of my relationships intact?"
- "Which friend is worth the occasional humble concession?"
- "Can I handle being slightly less chaotic if it means not alienating everyone?"

If the answer is "Yes" to any of these, congrats—you're on the path to semi-redemption.

Look, we both know you didn't pick up this book to become a saint, but if you've made it to this chapter, maybe a small part of you wonders if there's more to life than burning bridges. If so, these steps should help you *kind of* fix—or at least camouflage—your worst offenses. And if you decide to keep wreaking havoc instead, well… you do you. Just remember to send an apology text once in a while, it keeps everyone guessing.

42

SURVIVAL GUIDE FOR COLLATERAL DAMAGE

So, you've encountered someone who's an expert at everything this book so expertly teaches—congratulations (and condolences). If you suspect your friend, partner, coworker, or long-lost cousin has been studying these sabotage strategies, you might be in for some emotional whiplash. But fret not: here's a handy survival guide to help you keep your sanity (and maybe even salvage what's left of the relationship).

Step 1: Recognize the Warning Signs

You'll know you're dealing with a chaos aficionado when they:

- Arrive offensively late to every gathering, then depart early with no remorse.

- Interrupt your heartfelt stories to complain about their burnt toast.

- Perform the classic *+1 style* dinner approach: show up empty-handed and leave with leftovers.

Pro Tip: If they perfect the "I can't find my wallet" move at mealtime, they might be a full-on disciple of this book. Brace yourself.

Step 2: Establish (and Reinforce) Boundaries

You'll need boundaries so sturdy they rival fortress walls. Whether it's limiting how long you'll wait for them before starting dinner or politely shutting down their petty gossip, make your limits crystal clear.

Example:

- Time Limit: "If you're not here by 7:15, I'm going to start the movie without you."
- Gossip Cut-Off: "I'm not comfortable trash-talking Felicia. Pass the popcorn, please."

They'll be surprised when you don't indulge every chaotic whim—and that's a good thing.

Step 3: The Art of Detaching

Master the skill of detaching from their meltdown, one-upmanship, or guilt trips. Smile, nod, and exit stage left. If they're overshadowing your accomplishments or turning your success into their pity party, take a deep breath and remind yourself: *This is about them, not you.*

Example:

Them: "Wow, your promotion must be nice—but my car won't start."

You (calmly): "That sounds rough. Want to hear more about my new position later, or should I come back when you're ready?"

This gently underscores that they're making it about them, yet you're not playing along.

Step 4: Defend Your Wallet

Financial sabotage is a hallmark of chaos-lovers: skipping out on the bill, ordering lavishly, and sighing about their *forgotten* credit card. Protect your finances by establishing payment rules—split checks, separate bills, or use mobile pay before the meal begins.

Example:

- "Hey everyone, should we ask for separate checks as soon as we order? Easier that way, right?"

If they whine about your refusal to pay for their steak again, nod sympathetically and suggest the nearest ATM.

Step 5: Master the Minimal Response

When they corner you with a never-ending monologue, deploy minimal acknowledgment: short "uh-huhs" and distant smiles. No eye contact, no follow-up questions. This quietly signals you're not enthralled by their self-centered rant, and they might wrap it up sooner.

Pro Tip: If your phone politely *rings* mid-story, who are you to deny its urgent call?

Reflection Exercise:

- Which traits from this book's litany of annoyances have you encountered in your life?
- What boundaries or quick escapes can you set up to keep your own sanity?

- Are you enabling their behavior by letting them hog the spotlight, or are you gently calling them out?

Remember, protecting your peace isn't rude—it's survival.

Dealing with someone who's seemingly earned a PhD in *How to Lose Friends and Piss People Off* can feel like trying to salsa dance through a minefield. But with a clear set of boundaries, a couple of clever escape plans (and maybe the odd *urgent* text), you can dodge their worst antics—and still have fun. After all, life's too short to let anyone else's chaos hijack your good time.

CONCLUSION

You've made it to the end of *How to Lose Friends and Piss People Off*. If you've laughed, cringed, or thought, "Wait, do I do that?", then this book has done its job. While these exaggerated behaviors are meant to entertain, they also hold up a funhouse mirror to the quirks and habits we all share—some more than others.

Here's the thing: relationships are messy, and none of us get it right all the time. But hopefully, by leaning into the absurdity of these scenarios, you've found a new appreciation for the art of connection (or at least a better understanding of what *not* to do).

If you did recognize any of these traits in yourself, don't panic. It's never too late to course-correct—or, at the very least, to make light of your mistakes. And if you've bought this book as a gift for someone, well, good luck explaining why you thought it was perfect for them.

Remember: the goal of life isn't to lose friends and piss people off… but if you do it with style, at least it'll be memorable.

Thanks for reading, and may your future interactions be just a little less chaotic—or a lot more.

ACKNOWLEDGMENTS

To my friends and family: Thank you for the endless supply of comedic inspiration—no awkward silences or side-eyes needed. Just know that your everyday antics played a significant role in shaping these pages.

Special shout-out to my parents, whose unwavering belief in me has never gone unnoticed. Who would have guessed that your encouragement would lead me to writing an entire how-to guide on losing friends and pissing people off? It's reassuring to know I could write about something unorthodox and still get your seal of approval.

And to you, dear reader—especially if you've made it all the way here—I appreciate you more than you know. Whether you took this book seriously (please don't), bought it as a joke for a friend (yikes), or just needed a laugh at someone else's expense, thank you! I hope your newfound "skills" serve more as a cautionary tale than a roadmap for your friendships.

With gratitude,

Daajan

Daajan Bain is a first-time author, born on the Sunshine Coast, Australia, with a background in hospitality and short-term property management. In 2024, she embarked on her first solo backpacking adventure, exploring eight countries with nothing but a backpack. Along the way, she discovered that no matter the country, one thing remained true: at our core, we're all more alike than we realize—especially when it comes to the little habits that drive each other crazy.

The idea of *How to Lose Friends and Piss People Off* was sparked during an unexpected conversation with a family member—and possibly one too many encounters with people who really needed a hint. As she wrote, she soon realized these scenarios weren't just about others; many of them applied to her, too (which was both amusing and mildly concerning).

Daajan enjoys being in the garden, creating art, experimenting in the kitchen, and adopting more chickens than she originally intended. She also has a history of picking up hobbies only to abandon them shortly after, making her home an accidental museum of unfinished projects.

Despite the book's mischievous theme, she secretly hopes readers hold on to just enough friends to share a laugh and maybe even learn what *not* to do.

GLOSSARY

Backhanded Compliment:
A verbal gift wrapped in subtle shade. Example: "You look great for someone who clearly doesn't sleep much."

Bathroom Bandit:
A person who leaves behind empty toilet paper rolls, half-flushed disasters, and mysterious puddles around the sink. Known for their talent in turning a shared bathroom into a crime scene.

Blackhole:
A person who sucks up all attention, energy, and conversation without giving anything back. Once engaged, there is no escape, you will be trapped in their orbit of endless complaints and oversharing.

Boundary Breaker:
Someone who believes "What's mine is mine, and what's yours is also mine." Specializes in oversharing, uninvited visits, and borrowing without returning.

Couch Surfer:
A guest who arrives with no clear departure plan. Often claims they're "just crashing for a night" but mysteriously still occupies your living room three weeks later.

Fashionably Late:
The art of arriving not just late, but so late that the host is rethinking their entire relationship with you. Bonus points if you blame "traffic" while living two minutes away.

Ghosting:
The Houdini of communication. Involves disappearing from texts, calls, and group chats only to reappear weeks later with a casual, "What's up?"

Group Photo Menace:
A person who insists on retaking group pictures 50 times until they look flawless—at the expense of everyone else's dignity.

Micro-Manager Extraordinaire:
An overachiever in the field of nitpicking. Thrives on monitoring every move of their team to ensure maximum irritation.

One-Upper:
The storyteller who can't resist making your achievements sound insignificant.

Overstaying Guest:
A person who ignores every social cue and lingers well after the event has ended.

Rookie:
Someone new to social sabotage who hasn't yet mastered the art of being insufferable. Rookie mistakes include apologizing, showing up on time, and contributing to group plans.

Saboteur:
A master of ruining social interactions in ways both subtle and dramatic. Whether it's hogging conversations, forgetting to pay their share of dinner, or taking credit for someone else's joke, the true saboteur never misses a chance to derail an experience.

The Art of Gossip:
An ancient skill involving the unnecessary amplification of half-truths for maximum entertainment.

www.ingramcontent.com/pod-product-compliance
Lightning Source LLC
Chambersburg PA
CBHW071239070526
44583CB00017B/2258